T0059532

SOCIAL (*IN*)JUSTICE

SOCIAL (*IN*)JUSTICE

Why Many Popular Answers to Important Questions of Race, Gender, and Identity Are Wrong —and How to Know What's Right

A Reader-Friendly Remix of Cynical Theories

Helen Pluckrose and James Lindsay

Adapted by Rebecca Christiansen

Pitchstone Publishing
Durham, North Carolina

Pitchstone Publishing
Durham, North Carolina
www.pitchstonebooks.com

This book is based on *Cynical Theories: How Activist Scholarship Made Everything about Race, Gender, and Identity—and Why This Harms Everybody* by Helen Pluckrose and James Lindsay, first published by Pitchstone Publishing in 2020, and was adapted by Rebecca Christiansen.

Library of Congress Cataloging-in-Publication Data

Names: Christiansen, Rebecca, author. | Pluckrose, Helen, author. |
 Lindsay, James, author. | Pluckrose, Helen. Cynical theories.
Title: Social (in)justice : why many popular answers to important questions
 of race, gender, and identity are wrong-and how to know what's right : a
 reader-friendly remix of Cynical theories / Helen Pluckrose and James
 Lindsay ; adapted by Rebecca Christiansen.
Description: Durham, North Carolina : Pitchstone Publishing, [2022] | "This
 book is based on Cynical Theories: How Activist Scholarship Made
 Everything about Race, Gender, and Identity--and Why This Harms
 Everybody by Helen Pluckrose and James Lindsay, first published by
 Pitchstone Publishing in 2020"—Verso. | Includes bibliographical
 references. | Summary: "Argues that many popular approaches to questions
 of social justice are illiberal and offers an alternative vision for
 social justice based on liberal principles, adapted from the Wall Street
 Journal bestseller Cynical Theories"— Provided by publisher.
Identifiers: LCCN 2021028174 (print) | LCCN 2021028175 (ebook) | ISBN
 9781634312233 (hardcover) | ISBN 9781634312240 (ebook)
Subjects: LCSH: Social justice—Philosophy. | Postmodernism. | Philosophy,
 Modern—20th century.
Classification: LCC HM671 .C487 2022 (print) | LCC HM671 (ebook) | DDC
 303.3/7201—dc23
LC record available at https://lccn.loc.gov/2021028174
LC ebook record available at https://lccn.loc.gov/2021028175

For Generation Z who is our best hope.

CONTENTS

INTRODUCTION

Depending on your age and education, you've likely never come across a book quite like this before. At first glance, the subject may seem a bit unusual and unfamiliar, but our approach is really not that much different from other books you may have read in school or for pleasure. In many ways this book is like an introductory book on, say, world history, but rather than focusing on key people, events, innovations, and dates, and how they all acted together to affect and define the course of history, we're focusing on the evolution of a particular set of *ideas*, and how these ideas are affecting and defining the history we're living through today. As you will learn, how and whether these new ideas will define our future is largely up to the principles and positions we take now. The proliferation of this particular set of ideas presents a challenge to—and often directly conflicts with—another set of extremely important ideas collectively referred to as "liberalism." You may be surprised to learn that this word means something a little different than the way we usually hear it used in political discussions today. Indeed, liberalism is the bedrock on which modern societies in the West have been built and that continues to allow for so much human progress.

The exact story of how and why liberalism came to beat out many other ideas to become the foundational political philosophy in the West is beyond the scope of this book, but in the simplest terms, over the past two hundred years or so, most Western countries gradually came to realize that liberalism is the best political philosophy on which to build a modern civilization. There are many different political systems in Western countries, from the republics of the United States and France to the constitutional monarchy of the United Kingdom and Canada, but they're all underpinned by the same liberal values.

Some of those liberal values are:

- Democracy
- Limited government
- Separation of church and state
- Universal human rights
- Equality for women, racial minorities, and LGBT people
- Freedom of expression
- Respect for the value of differing opinions and honest debate

Today, these values might seem like basic common sense. But they should not be seen as a given, or be taken for granted. They didn't begin to take hold until the 1700s, during the period known as the Enlightenment, and it's taken centuries of struggle against superstition, theocracy, slavery, patriarchy, colonialism, and fascism to realize them to the extent we have. This extent is considerable but not perfect. The aim for a golden age of science, reason, and individual rights based on beliefs in a shared objective reality and shared universal humanity is the ongoing project of the Enlightenment and liberalism.

In the 1960s, a new idea emerged in academia that would question everything, including the very basis of liberal societies. This idea is known as postmodernism, a philosophical, artistic, and literary movement that is extremely skeptical—so skeptical that it doesn't believe in objective truth or knowledge. Sounds crazy, but it's true. Postmodernism believes everything is corrupted by politics and political power, even knowledge itself.

Postmodern ideas have formed a broad literature of its own called *Theory*—think of Theory like postmodernism's body of religious texts. Since the 1960s, Theory has spread through governments, corporations, and primary, secondary, and postsecondary education. In more recent years, Theory has spawned a movement of activists who weaponize postmodernism in pursuit of "social justice." In fact, you have almost certainly encountered *a lot* of Theory over the past few years, even if it wasn't ever directly presented as such.

The term "social justice" has had a lot of different meanings. In 1971, the liberal progressive philosopher John Rawls developed a philosophical theory on how a socially just society might be organized. He thought a socially just society would be one where anyone would be equally happy to be born into any social milieu or identity group, whether at the top or bottom of the society, because even those at the bottom would be thriving and injustices like discrimination would be exceptionally rare or entirely absent.

The most visible and popular movement taking up the charge of social justice today uses postmodern Theory to pursue social justice. It calls its ideology—a system of opinions and beliefs that aim both to explain and change society—"Social Justice," the "Social Justice Movement," or, sometimes more specifically, "Critical Social Justice." Many people, including its critics, call it being "Woke" (due to its belief that it is "awake" to "systemic" injustice). This is the Theory you are no doubt regularly encountering—at school, at work, online, or simply out and about with friends—and you may even be a bit baffled by it all. For the sake of clarity—and because it also derives from another twentieth-century tradition called "Critical Theory"—we'll refer to this particular Theory-based movement as "Critical Social Justice," and we'll refer to the broader and more general idea that everyone deserves equal rights and opportunities as "social justice."

Here, it's important to note that the modifier "critical" in "Critical Social Justice" has a specific academic meaning related to "critique" and thus does not imply objective analysis as in "critical thinking." Instead, it refers to a specific and *illiberal* approach that does not believe in objectivity and loosely tries to explain how society fails to be perfect or even a utopia.

Many people have strong opinions about "Wokeness," or Critical Social Justice, perhaps even you. Here's our position, which will inform much of this book: we oppose Critical Social Justice because we believe in social justice. Put another way, we believe that Critical Social Justice offers the wrong answers to important questions about race, gender, and identity and that it does not offer a path to true social justice. Further, we believe that the Critical Social Justice approach runs counter to many of the core liberal values outlined above; that rights belong to individuals, not groups; and that ideals such as truth, objectivity, and merit should be central to securing those rights—and justice. That is, we advocate for a fairer society that minimizes the impacts of identity-based discrimination and prejudice, but we reject both the push for group-based rights and the methods by which the Critical Social Justice movement seeks to achieve them.

Almost every day, a story comes out about somebody who has been fired, "cancelled," or subjected to a public shaming on social media for saying or doing something interpreted as sexist, racist, or homophobic. Sometimes the accusations are warranted, and we can comfort ourselves knowing that a bigot—someone, of course, totally unlike us—is receiving the punishment she "deserves." But increasingly, it feels like anyone, even a firm believer in universal liberty and equality, could inadvertently say or do something the Critical Social Justice movement doesn't like and face devastating consequences.

At best, this has a chilling effect on our culture of free expression, a core principle of liberalism that has produced much knowledge and moral progress over the last two centuries. At worst, it's a malicious form of bullying, and when institutional-ized, a kind of totalitarianism.

In any case, it's not liberal; it's *illiberal*.

These changes stem from a very peculiar view of the world—one that speaks its own language. When Critical Social Justice scholars and activists speak of "racism," for example, they aren't referring to prejudice on the grounds of race. They have their own definition, which can be summarized as: "a ra-cialized system that permeates all interactions in society yet is largely invisible except to those who experience it or who have been trained in the proper methods that allow them to see it."

This very specialized usage of the word inevitably confuses the average person. Many of us can sense that something has gone wrong, but it can be difficult to formulate a response, es-pecially when objections are often misunderstood or misrepre-sented as opposition to genuine social justice.

Aside from their own language, these scholars and activ-ists also seem to have their own culture. They're obsessed with power, language, knowledge, and the relationships between them. They detect power dynamics in every interaction, utter-ance, and cultural artifact. Their worldview makes everything into a political struggle revolving around identity markers like race, sex, gender, sexuality, and many others.

As experienced travelers know, there's more to communi-cating in a different culture than learning the language. You also have to learn the idioms, implications, cultural references, and etiquette. Often, we don't just need a translator but an *in-*

terpreter, someone who knows both sets of customs, to help us communicate effectively. That's why we wrote this book. It will guide you through the language and culture of this world, which remains alien to many, chart a history of the evolution of these ideas, and propose a way for those who believe in liberal values to counter them.

Some Critical Social Justice advocates will insist that those with a liberal mind-set are just reactionary right-wingers who don't believe in the injustice experienced by marginalized people. Others will reject the liberal, empirical (evidence-based), and rational stance on the issues as an outdated delusion that centers white, male, Western, and heterosexual ("straight") constructions of knowledge and maintains an unjust status quo. "The master's tools will never dismantle the master's house," they will tell us.

While that statement itself probably isn't true, it does accurately represent our intentions. We don't want to dismantle liberal societies and empirical and rational concepts of knowledge. We want to continue the amazing advances for social justice that they have brought. The "master's" house is a good one—the problem has been limited access to it. Liberalism increases access to a solid structure that can shelter and empower everyone. Tearing the liberal house down might make equal access quicker and easier to achieve, but equal access to a pile of rubble isn't a worthy goal.

Wherever you encounter Critical Social Justice ideas, whether in school, at work, at home, online, or among your friends, it's important to keep an open mind and consider each idea on its own merits, just as we hope you'll keep an open mind to the ideas we present in this book. Even if you find you strongly disagree with most Critical Social Justice ideas, as we ourselves do, remember that those who believe them aren't enemies to be debated and defeated. They're still your classmates, peers, co-workers, friends, and family members, or maybe even your teachers or bosses. You likely have a lot in common. Even so, you may at times feel alienated and misunderstood, but lashing out in anger or frustration is the wrong response. Approaching with *understanding* is the right response. This includes having a principled position of your own toward social justice on which to stand—ideally one based on traditional liberal values. Doing so can establish a path for having productive and ideologically diverse conversations about these important issues. We hope this book will provide you with some of the knowledge and tools needed for having such conversations—and even for figuring out your own principles and beliefs.

Those with a Critical Social Justice worldview and those with a liberal worldview often see the same problems. After all, Critical Social Justice activists want a fair world—the same thing we want. They just have ideas of how to get there that are different from our own and may not understand why we as liberals argue not only that their ideas won't work but also that their ideas will ultimately do more harm than good.

If both sides listen to each other in good faith, however, we can find common ground. It's not always easy, but keeping an open mind and engaging in open dialogue is always the correct path.

1 POSTMODERNISM
Questioning Knowledge and Power

In the 1960s, a radical new way to think about the world and our place in it was introduced in France. Leading figures behind this new way of thinking were Michel Foucault, Jacques Derrida, and Jean-François Lyotard, among others. Although most people in the English-speaking world probably haven't heard of these French Theorists, the change they inspired—postmodernism—revolutionized social philosophy, the study of society and the institutions and human relationships that form it. Over the decades, postmodernism has not only dramatically altered what and how we think, but also how we think about thinking itself. It has led many people to question how we know what we believe we know and even if we can truly know *anything* at all.

Whoa.

So what is postmodernism, really? The online *Encyclopedia Britannica* defines it as a late 20th-century movement characterized by broad skepticism, subjectivism, or relativism; a general suspicion of reason; and an acute sensitivity to the role of ideology in asserting and maintaining political and economic power.

Postmodernism first appeared in the arts around 1940, but by the late 1960s, it was in the humanities and social sciences, including fields like psychoanalysis, linguistics, philosophy, history, and sociology. The early thinkers in these fields drew from their precursors in surrealist art, revolutionary politics, and antirealist philosophy. ("Antirealist" philosophy says that while the real world might be out there, there's no meaningful connection between it and our claims of knowledge about it—knowledge is just *ideas* expressed in *words*, not reality or even a truly meaningful description of reality.)

Since we're focusing on the aspects of postmodern thought that have been applied to the real world and become socially and culturally powerful today, this chapter won't be a complete summary of postmodernism. We'll highlight some underlying themes of postmodernism that drive today's Critical Social Justice activism, shape educational theory and practice, and dominate our current conversations about social justice.

The Roots, Principles, and Themes of Postmodernism

Like all intellectual movements, postmodernism emerged in a specific social and political context. To understand the modern context from which it emerged, however, we first need to understand a bit about the past. Among other things, we need to understand the role skepticism, or a questioning attitude, has played in shaping history since the 1500s, when Christianity splintered into different sects during the period known as the Reformation. These new groups all challenged both the old ways and each other. By the end of the sixteenth century, treatises against atheism also began to appear, which suggests that some people in that era had even stopped believing in God.

Up until this time, most scientific knowledge in the West had come from the ancient Greeks. But in the 1600s, medicine and anatomy underwent a revolution, and Europeans quickly learned a lot about the human body. Other revolutionary advances were made in mathematics, physics, and astronomy. Collectively, these developments played a crucial role in the rise of Enlightenment thought, which broke away from the then-dominant religious narratives and spread throughout Europe in the 1700s. This Enlightenment thought included the liberal ideas and principles on which modern Western societies came to be based. These developments, in turn, led to the emergence of the scientific method in the 1800s, which was centered on skepticism, questioning conventional wisdom, and the need for increasingly rigorous testing and falsification—the process of attempting to prove things false.

A series of rapid developments in the early 1900s, including increasing political volatility and eventually war across Europe, contributed to changing ideas about class and gender and gave rise to a strain of thought and art that came to be known as "modernism." Products of this philosophical, artistic, and cultural movement included a strange mixture of pessimistic

skepticism about reality and progress and a focus on subjectivity, with an overly confident belief in the individual and universal truths and the potential of innovation.

By the middle of the twentieth century, a number of profound social and political changes had happened in a very
short time. The First and Second World Wars shook Europe's
confidence in the notion of progress and made people wary of
the power of technology, since it had been used to commit so
many atrocities in the wars themselves, in Nazi Germany, and
under Communism, the official state ideology of the Soviet
Union based on the revolutionary socialist ideas of German
philosopher Karl Marx. Left-wing intellectuals across Europe
grew suspicious of liberalism and Western civilization, which
had allowed the rise of fascism, a totalitarian and authoritarian
ideology, in Germany, Italy, and elsewhere. At the same time,
the horrific effects of Communist ideology in the Soviet Union
during that period could no longer be denied, even by those
on the political and cultural left. The same could be said for
colonialism, which was no longer seen as morally justifiable
or defensible as European colonies, such as British and French
colonies in Africa, Asia, and elsewhere, successfully fought for
and gained independence.

Meanwhile, technology and the mass production of con-
sumer goods fueled a renewed hunger for art, music, and enter-
tainment after the strict rationing and deprivations caused by
the Second World War. This sparked conservative fears that society was degenerating into an artificial, hedonistic, consumer-
ist world of fantasy and play, while significant social justice ac-

tivism was met with other types of fears and hostile resistance. In the United States, for example, the Civil Rights Movement that began in the 1950s reached its peak in the 1960s, with African Americans fighting for and winning equal rights under the law despite often-violent opposition. On the heels of those important victories, activism by and on behalf of women and lesbian, gay, bisexual, and transgender (LGBT) people took hold and slowly began to gain broad cultural support.

Throughout this period of turmoil and transition, more people from around the world started to migrate to Western countries, prompting those in the West to gradually pay more attention to racial and cultural inequalities and, particularly, to the ways in which structures of power had contributed to them. At the same time, science's role in enabling, producing, and justifying the previously impossible horrors of the preceding decades was interrogated as well.

In this context, there was a shift in how many scholars and academics in the West came to view the world and its systems—from a belief in human progress based on science, reason, and liberal principles, to a belief that everything should be eyed with suspicion and skepticism, including the very tools that had led to unprecedented human progress. Put another way, modernism gave birth to postmodernism.

Postmodernism is radically skeptical of just about everything. It's skeptical of science and other culturally dominant ways of deciding what is "true," and of the grand, sweeping explanations that support them. It called those *metanarratives*—a kind of cultural mythology that, in the eyes of postmodern thinkers, demonstrated how shortsighted and arrogant humans are in thinking that simple narratives could explain the world. Postmodernism didn't invent skepticism, but it took it to extremes by doubting that there was any such thing as knowable truth that was not thoroughly embedded in cultural norms and beliefs.

According to the reason- and science-based thinking that came out of the Enlightenment and on which more than two centuries of human progress have relied, however, objective reality can be known and discovered. Indeed, we built our modern world using knowledge about objective reality produced by the scientific method, and we continue to do so today. In the postmodern view, though, reality is the product of our socialization and lived experiences, as constructed by systems of language.

The sociologist Steven Seidman recognized this change in thinking in 1994: "A broad social and cultural shift is taking place in Western societies. The concept of the 'postmodern' captures at least certain aspects of this social change." Walter Truett Anderson, writing in 1996, put it more strongly: "We are in the midst of a great, confusing, stressful and enormously promising historical transition, and it has to do with a change not so much in *what* we believe but *how* we believe. . . . People all over the world are making such shifts in belief—to be more precise, shifts in belief about belief."

What Seidman and Anderson are describing here are changes in *epistemology*—that is, changes in how we obtain and understand knowledge.

Two Principles and Four Themes

Postmodern thinkers rejected modernism and Enlightenment thought in strikingly different ways, but we can spot a few consistent themes and two core principles.

These principles are:

- **The postmodern knowledge principle:** Radical skepticism about whether objective knowledge or truth is obtainable and a commitment to cultural constructivism.

- **The postmodern political principle:** A belief that society is made up of systems of power and hierarchies, which decide what can be known and how.

The four major themes of postmodernism are

1. The blurring of boundaries
2. The power of language
3. Cultural relativism
4. The loss of the individual and the universal

Together, these six major concepts help us identify postmodern thinking and understand how it operates. These are the core principles of postmodern Theory, which have remained largely unchanged as postmodernism evolved from its pessimistic beginnings to today's strident activism. We'll explore all of these in detail, and see how they arose in the humanities over the last century and developed into the postmodernist Critical Social Justice scholarship, activism, and culture we see today.

The Postmodern Knowledge Principle

Radical skepticism as to whether objective knowledge or truth
is obtainable and a commitment to cultural constructivism

Instead of seeing objective truth as something that can be discovered through experimentation and falsification, postmodernism exaggerates a small kernel of truth—that our ability to *know* is limited by our cultural viewpoints and language—by saying that *all* claims of "truth" are biased cultural constructs. In this view, the scientific method isn't seen as a better way of producing and legitimizing knowledge than any other, but as just one approach among many, as corrupted by biased reasoning as any other. This is called *cultural constructivism/constructionism* or *social constructivism/constructionism*.

Cultural constructivism doesn't necessarily say that reality is *literally* created by cultural beliefs—for example, it doesn't say that when we believed the Sun went around the Earth, our beliefs had influence over the solar system and its dynamics. Instead, it would say that humans are so tied into their cultural frameworks that all truth or knowledge claims are reflections of those frameworks. It would say that we collectively *decided* that it's "true" that the Earth goes around the Sun, but that if we belonged to a culture that produced and legitimated knowledge differently, then it might be "true" that, say, the Sun goes around the Earth (even though it doesn't), and those who disagreed would be considered "crazy" in that culture, just as we would view someone who believes the opposite today to be "crazy."

Our perceived reality is influenced by our cultural norms,

but that doesn't mean that truth is best understood primarily as a product of cultural norms. The postmodern approach to knowledge might acknowledge that objective reality exists "out there," but it focuses on the barriers to knowing that reality by examining cultural biases and assumptions and theorizing about how they work.

French philosopher Michel Foucault—a central figure of postmodernism—was interested in the relationships between *discourse* (ways of talking about things), the production of knowledge, and power. He explored these ideas at length throughout the 1960s, in such influential works as *Madness and Civilization* (1961), *The Birth of the Clinic* (1963), *The Order of Things* (1966), and *The Archaeology of Knowledge* (1969).

For Foucault, a statement communicates not just information, but also the rules and conditions of a discourse, which are set by those with power in the relevant culture. For example, if you tell a friend that you think Iron Man is the best Avenger, you're not just communicating that you like Iron Man—you're revealing your personal politics and position in society and lending support to the messages that Iron Man promotes. You're also implying what values you *don't* support.

Sociopolitical power is the ultimate determiner of what is "true" in Foucault's analysis. For him, whether a truth claim is actually true or not is less interesting and important than the power dynamics that led to people believing it is true. Foucault was so interested in the concept of how power influences what is considered knowledge that in 1981 he coined the term "power/knowledge" to describe the link between powerful discourses and what is understood to be known.

In his book *The Order of Things,* Foucault argues against objective notions of truth and suggests we think instead in terms of "regimes of truth," which change according to the specific *episteme* (knowledge set that grounds a discourse) of each culture and time. Foucault adopted the position that there are no fundamental principles by which to discover truth and that all knowledge is "local" to the knower—the postmodern knowledge principle.

Foucault didn't deny that reality exists, but he doubted that humans could transcend our cultural biases enough to get at it. He thought every statement about reality is a political statement. You can recognize the influence of his thought today, when people make the political implications of a thing so central to how we think and talk about it—for instance, when the political implications of Iron Man, the billionaire heir of a weapons company, become more important than his storyline or heroic actions.

The main takeaway from this is that postmodern skepticism is more than just reasonable doubt. The kind of skepticism employed in the sciences asks, "How can I be sure this is true?" or, even more importantly, "How might this be false?" and scientists will only tentatively accept propositions that survive repeated attempts to prove them false. These propositions are made into models, which are used to explain and predict phenomena and are judged by their accuracy. Scientific models change when new information or evidence arises. This intellectual humility in science leads postmodern philosophers to say (wrongly) that scientists therefore can't say they *know* anything or that there are any scientific *truths*, because they might realize later that they were wrong.

The skepticism common among postmodernists is referred to as "*radical* skepticism." It says, "All knowledge is constructed: what's interesting is theorizing about why knowledge got constructed this way." What is true and how we know it is true is less interesting to them than finding out who it benefits to say something is "true." Postmodernism sees knowledge as intrinsically political.

The postmodern view insists that scientific reasoning is just another *metanarrative*—a sweeping, oversimplified explanation of how things work. This is wrong.

The Postmodern Political Principle

A belief that society is formed of power and hierarchies, which decide what can be known and how

In postmodernism, power and knowledge are seen as inextricably entwined—most explicitly in Foucault's work, which refers to knowledge as "power/knowledge." Another French postmodernist, Jean-François Lyotard, describes a "strict interlinkage" between the language of science and that of politics and ethics, and another, Jacques Derrida, was interested in the power dynamics of superiority and subordination in language. Similarly, two more, Gilles Deleuze and Félix Guattari, saw humans as coded within various systems of power and constraint, free to operate only within capitalism and the flow of money.

These thinkers argued that the powerful organize society to benefit themselves and help them keep their power, both intentionally and inadvertently. They do this by slanting the way we talk about certain things and creating social rules that are viewed as common sense. Power is constantly reinforced through the discourses that society deems legitimate. Examples include the expectation of civility and reasoned debate, appeals to objective evidence, and even rules of grammar and syntax.

For example, simply asking someone to provide evidence and reasoning for their claims—for example, that the Sun revolves around the Earth, or that Captain Marvel is the best Avenger—will be seen as a demand to comply with a system of discourses built by powerful people who valued these approaches and designed them to exclude alternative means of communicating and producing "knowledge." In other words, postmodern Theory believes science was organized in a way that serves the interests of the powerful people who established it—white Western men—and bars others from participating.

In Marxist theory, power is believed to be enforced from the top onto those at the bottom. In postmodern Theory, power permeates all levels of society and gets reinforced by everyone through routine interactions, expectations, and social conditioning. It's the social system and its inherent power dynamics that are seen as the causes of oppression. The individuals involved don't necessarily even have to hold a single oppressive view. As well, the system of oppression isn't seen as a consciously coordinated, patriarchal, white supremacist, heteronormative conspiracy. Instead, postmodern Theory sees this oppression as the inevitable result of self-perpetuating systems that privilege some groups over others. The postmodernist view sort of looks like a conspiracy theory—but one without conspirators, since there are no coordinated actors pulling the strings.

Because they focused on self-perpetuating systems of power, few of the original postmodern Theorists advocated any specific political actions, preferring instead to playfully disrupt or indulge in pessimistic despair. They didn't really believe meaningful change was possible. Nevertheless, the overtly left-wing idea that oppressive power structures constrain humanity runs throughout postmodernism. This implies an ethical duty to deconstruct, challenge, problematize (find and exaggerate the problems within), and resist ways of thinking that support power and the language that perpetuates it.

Foucault was explicit about the ever-present danger of oppressive systems:

> My point is not that everything is bad, but that everything is dangerous, which is not exactly the same as bad. If everything is dangerous, then we always have something to do. So, my position leads not to apathy but to a hyper- and pessimistic activism. I think that the ethico-political choice we have to make every day is to determine which is the main danger.

The postmodern approach to social critique is to make their ideas intangible, because then they're unfalsifiable—that is, they can't be disproved. Due to postmodernism's rejection of objective truth and reason, it can't be argued with. The postmodern perception, Lyotard writes, makes no claim to be true: "Our hypothesis . . . should not be accorded predictive value in relation to reality, but strategic value in relation to the question raised." Postmodern Theory seeks to be strategically useful in bringing about its own aims, not factually true about reality.

This leads to the four main themes: the blurring of boundaries, the power of language, cultural relativism, and the loss of the individual and the universal in favor of group identity.

1. The Blurring of Boundaries

Radical skepticism toward objective truth and knowledge, combined with the belief that systems are constructed in the service of power, results in a suspicion of the boundaries and categories we have generally accepted as true. These include the boundaries between objective and subjective, as well as those between science and the arts (especially for Lyotard), the natural and the artificial, high and low culture, man and other animals, man and machine (for Deleuze), and different understandings of sexuality and gender as well as health and sickness (see, especially, Foucault). All of these thinkers treat the boundaries between these things as fluid.

2. The Power of Language

In postmodern thought, language has enormous power to control society and how we think, so it's inherently dangerous. In 1967, Jacques Derrida published three texts—*Of Grammatology, Writing and Difference,* and *Speech and Phenomena*—in which he introduced a concept that would become very influential in postmodernism: deconstruction.

In these works, Derrida rejects the commonsense idea that words ("signifiers") refer straightforwardly to things in the real world (the "signified"). Instead, he insists that words refer only to other words and to the ways in which they differ from one another. For example, his style of thought would argue that a word like "house" can only be understood in relation to the words "hut" (smaller) and "mansion" (larger), or "building site" (place where a house might be built) and "empty lot" (place where a house isn't), and that beyond these kinds of comparisons, the word "house" has no meaning. This is what Derrida meant in his famous and often-mistranslated phrase, "there is nothing [read: no meaning] outside of text."

Additionally, for Derrida, the speaker's intent has no more authority than the hearer's interpretation. If someone says that certain features of a culture can generate problems, and I choose to interpret this statement as a dog whistle about the inferiority of that culture and take offense, Derridean analysis would deny the possibility that my offense came from a misunderstanding of what had been said. This comes from Derrida's use of Roland Barthes' concept of "the death of the author," a literary theory that removes the author and their intent from consideration when analyzing a text's meaning.

Derrida's solution to keeping discourses from creating and maintaining oppression is to read "deconstructively," by looking for internal inconsistencies that reveal a text's true intentions when the words are examined closely enough (or with an agenda). Deconstructive approaches to language often look like nitpicking at words in order to deliberately miss the point.

3. Cultural Relativism

Because postmodern Theory believes truth and knowledge are constructed by the dominant discourses within a society, and because we can't examine our own system and categories from the outside, it insists that no one set of cultural norms is any better than another. Any critique made by someone outside of a culture will be incorrect at best and immoral at worst, since it presupposes your culture to be objectively superior.

For example, a wealthy person's critique of society will always be seen as being colored by their privilege. It will be potentially dismissed because it will be assumed to be ignorant of the realities of oppression, or just an attempt to serve the critic's own interests. The postmodern belief that individuals enact discourses of power depending on where they stand in relation to power means that cultural critique can only be effectively wielded by the marginalized or oppressed.

4. The Loss of the Individual and the Universal

To postmodern Theorists, the individual is a product of powerful discourses and culturally constructed knowledge. They view the concept of the universal—whether a biological universal or an ethical universal, such as equal rights, freedoms, and opportunities for all individuals regardless of class, race, gender, or sexuality—as naive at best. At worst, it's yet another exercise in power-knowledge, an attempt to enforce dominant discourses. The postmodern view largely rejects both the smallest unit of society—the individual—and the largest—humanity. Instead, it focuses on sets of people who are understood to be positioned in the same way—originally by nation, time period, and social or economic class, and later by race, sex, or sexuality, for example—and who have the same experiences and perceptions due to this social positioning.

Isn't Postmodernism Dead?

A lot of thinkers today believe that postmodernism has died out. We don't think it has. We think it has merely matured, mutated, and evolved (at least twice since the 1960s) and that the two principles and four themes are still pervasive and culturally influential. Theory is intact, although the ways in which its core principles and themes are presented, used, and interacted with have changed significantly over the last fifty years. Its current application is what concerns us most.

There are many arguments about when exactly postmodernism allegedly died. What we call postmodern Theory's *high deconstructive phase* burnt itself out by the mid-1980s, but did postmodernism and Theory end there? No. Far from dying out, these ideas evolved and diversified into distinct strands. They became more goal- and action-oriented by combining with another school of thought called Critical Theory, which was made especially by and for radical activists. We call the next wave of activism-scholarship *applied postmodernism*, and we'll dive into that next.

2 POSTMODERNISM'S APPLIED TURN
Making Oppression Real

Once postmodernism burst onto the intellectual scene in the late 1960s, it became wildly fashionable among leftist and left-leaning academics. As the intellectual fad grew, its recruits set to work producing radically skeptical Theory, in which Western knowledge and ways of obtaining knowledge—including our assumption that objective knowledge is even possible—were criticized and dismantled. The postmodernists sought to make our ways of understanding, approaching, and living in the world and in societies seem absurd.

This approach had its limits. Endless dismantling and deconstruction were doomed to consume them in nihilistic despair, a sense that all is useless and pointless. Theory was a rebel without a cause—it needed something to do. Because of its morally and politically charged core, it applied itself to the problem it saw at the core of society: unjust access to power.

A new wave of Theorists in the late 1980s and early 1990s created a diverse set of highly politicized and actionable postmodern Theories that included some elements of Critical Theory. We call this more recent development *applied postmodernism*. (In fact, an academic term for what we call "applied postmodernism" is *critical constructivism*. This is the cultural constructivist theme of postmodernism combined with the revolutionary and reconstructionist aims of the "New Left," which took inspiration from German-American political philosopher Herbert Marcuse and Critical Theory.) These applied postmodernists came from different fields, but their ideas were similar and provided a more user-friendly approach than the old postmodernism. During this turn, Theory mutated into a handful of Theories—postcolonial, queer, and critical race—that were put to work in the world to deconstruct social injustice.

Think of postmodernism as a kind of fast-evolving virus. Its original and purest form couldn't spread from the academy to the general population because it was so difficult to grasp and so far removed from social realities. In its mutated form, it was able to spread, leaping the "species" gap from academics to activists to everyday people as it became increasingly graspable and actionable and therefore more contagious.

The new strains of Theory are far less playful and far more confident in their own metanarratives. They have a practical aim that was absent before: to reconstruct society in the image of Critical Social Justice.

The Mutation of Theory

Between the late 1980s and roughly 2010, Theory developed its underlying concepts—that objective reality cannot be known, that "truth" is socially constructed, and that knowledge protects and advances the interests of the privileged—and formed entirely new fields of scholarship. These new disciplines, known as "(Critical) Social Justice scholarship," co-opted the notion of social justice from the civil rights movements and other liberal and progressive theories.

This all began in earnest just as legal equality had largely been achieved and antiracist, feminist, and LGBT activism began to produce diminishing returns. Now that racial and sexual discrimination in the workplace was illegal and homosexuality was decriminalized throughout the West, the main barriers to social equality in the West were lingering prejudices in attitudes, assumptions, expectations, and language. For those tackling these more obscure problems, postmodern Theory might have been an ideal tool—except that its deconstructive, indiscriminate radical skepticism and unpalatable nihilism made it unfit for any productive purpose.

The new forms of Theory arose within postcolonialism, black feminism (a branch of feminism pioneered by African American scholars who focused on race as well as gender), intersectional feminism, critical race (legal) Theory, and queer Theory. Scholars in these fields argued that, while postmodernism could help reveal the socially constructed nature of knowledge and the associated "problematics," it wasn't compatible with social activism. Some of the new Theorists criticized their forebears for being white, male, wealthy, and Western enough to be able to afford to deconstruct identity and identity-based oppression, because society was already set up for their benefit. As a result, while the new Theorists retained much postmodern Theory, they did not toss aside all ideas about the existence of such things as stable identity and objective truth, arguing that though many things might not be objectively real, oppression definitely is.

The original Theorists were content to observe, bemoan, and play word games; the new ones wanted to reorder society. If legitimizing bad discourses causes social injustice, the new Theorists reasoned, social justice can be achieved by delegitimizing them and replacing them with better discourses. Social sciences and humanities scholars who took Theoretical approaches began to form a left-wing moral community—a network of people who support one another in pursuit of a common moral goal—more interested in advocating for particular views than studying them objectively.

We usually see this kind of thing in churches, not in colleges or universities.

A New Default View

The new Theories retained a few core postmodern ideas:

- Knowledge is a construct of power.
- The categories into which we organize people and phenomena are constructed in the service of that power.

- Language is inherently dangerous and unreliable.

- The knowledge claims and values of all cultures are equally valid and only people who belong to those cultures can critique them.

- Collective experience trumps both individuality and universality.

Strangely, it's not uncommon for academics who use the postmodern knowledge and political principles in their work to disparage postmodernism and insist that they don't use it in their work. But whether we call it "postmodernism," "applied postmodernism," "Theory," or anything else, the conception of society based on the postmodern knowledge and political principles has flourished within many identity- and culture-based "studies" fields. These fields influence the social sciences and professional programs like education, law, psychology, and social work, and have been carried by activists and media into the broader culture.

Postmodernism has become applicable and, therefore, accessible to both activists and the general public.

Applying the Inapplicable

In the early 1600s, just as the Enlightenment began revolutionizing human thought in Europe, a number of thinkers of the time started to grapple with a new problem: radical doubt—a belief that there's no rational basis to believe *anything*.

Most famous among them was the French mathematician,

scientist, and philosopher René Descartes. In 1637, he first wrote the phrase, "*Je pense, donc je suis*," in *Discourse on the Method*—or, in English, "I think, therefore I am." This was Descartes' response to the deconstructive power that Enlightenment skepticism introduced to the world.

Something similar happened centuries later, in the 1980s. Faced with the far more intense deconstructive power of postmodern radical skepticism, an emerging band of cultural Theorists found themselves in a similar crisis. Liberal activism had won tremendous successes, but the nihilistic despair of postmodernism wasn't producing further change.

The answer to this problem would require an adaptation of Descartes' famous meditation. For him, the ability to think implied existence—if you can think, then *something* must be real. For the activist-scholars of the 1980s, the suffering associated with oppression implied the existence of something that could suffer and a mechanism by which that suffering can occur. "I think, therefore I am" became "I experience oppression, therefore I am . . . and so are dominance and oppression."

The Postmodern Principles and Themes in Application

Applied postmodernism retained the two postmodern principles at its core. They are so significant we will share them again.

The postmodern knowledge principle: Radical skepticism about whether objective knowledge or truth is obtainable and a commitment to cultural constructivism.

The postmodern political principle: A belief that society is formed of systems of power and hierarchies, which decide what can be known and how.

The first princinple—a denial of objective knowledge or truth and commitment to cultural constructivism, and belief that what we call "truth" is nothing more than a reflection of the culture calling it that—was largely retained, with one important difference: under applied postmodern thought, identity and oppression based on identity are treated as known features of objective reality.

For example, critical legal scholar Kimberlé Crenshaw, author of the groundbreaking 1991 essay "Mapping the Margins: Intersectionality, Identity Politics, and Violence against Women of Color," admired the deconstructive potential of postmodern Theory and centered it in her new "intersectional" framework for addressing discrimination against women of color. At the same time, she wanted to keep the idea of race and gender as social constructs, as well as assert that some people were discriminated against on the grounds of their racial or sexual identities.

What about the second principle? It has also been kept. In fact, the belief that the powerful form society to benefit themselves and decide what can be known and how, is central to the advocacy of identity politics, whose political aim is to dismantle this system in the name of Critical Social Justice.

The four key themes of postmodern thought also survived into the applied postmodern turn.

1. The Blurring of Boundaries

This theme shows up the most in postcolonial and queer Theories, which both explicitly center on ideas of fluidity, ambiguity, indefinability, and hybridity—all of which blur or even demolish the boundaries between categories. Their tactic of "disrupting binaries" follows from Derrida's work on the hierarchical nature and meaninglessness of linguistic constructions. This doesn't really show up in critical race Theory, which can be quite black-and-white (pun intended), but the intersectional feminist element of critical race Theory tries to be inclusive of "different ways of knowing."

2. The Power of Language

The power and danger of language are foregrounded in all the newer applied postmodern Theories. Scholars scrutinize language closely and interpret it according to Theoretical frameworks. For example, popular movies are watched "closely" for problematic portrayals and then disparaged, even if their themes are mostly consistent with Critical Social Justice. The idea that words are powerful and dangerous has now become widespread in this age of safe spaces, microaggressions, and trigger warnings.

3. Cultural Relativism

Cultural relativism is most obvious in postcolonial Theory, but since the West is almost universally viewed as the ultimate oppressive power structure, cultural relativism is now a norm in all applied postmodern Theories. This relativism is also central to the different knowledges and morality ascribed to different identity groups.

4. The Loss of the Individual and the Universal

The intense focus on identity and identity politics means that the individual and the universal are devalued. Mainstream liberalism focuses on achieving universal human rights and access to opportunities, to allow each individual to fulfill her potential. Applied postmodern scholarship and activism is skeptical of these values and even openly hostile to them. Its advocates see mainstream liberalism as complacent, naive, or indifferent about the deeply engrained prejudices, assumptions, and biases that limit and constrain people with marginalized identities. The "individual," to them, is seen mostly as the sum total of the identity groups to which the person in question belongs.

The Emergence of Social Justice Scholarship

These changes may not seem like enough to consider Theory a serious departure from postmodernism, but they're a big deal. By dropping the ironic playfulness and meaninglessness of high-deconstructive postmodernism and by becoming goal-oriented, Theory went from merely describing the way things are, to making prescriptions for how they ought to be. If "the truth" is only true because we privilege the discourses of straight, white, wealthy, Western men, applied Theory says this can be challenged by empowering marginalized identity groups and insisting their voices take precedence.

This belief amplified identity politics to such an extent that it even led to concepts like "research justice." This alarming proposal demands that scholars cite women and minorities in their research—and minimize citations of white Western men—because research that values evidence and reasoned argument is an unfairly privileged cultural construct of white Westerners. Therefore, in this view, it's a moral obligation to share the prestige of academia with "other forms of research," including superstition, spiritual beliefs, cultural traditions and beliefs, identity-based experiences, and emotional responses.

Since these methods can be applied to virtually anything, a vast body of identity-based fields has emerged since roughly 2010. These fields use their own approaches to *epistemology* (the ways in which knowledge is produced): there's feminist epistemology, critical race epistemology, postcolonial epistemology, and queer epistemology, along with the broader "epistemic justice," "epistemic oppression," "epistemic exploitation," and "epistemic violence."

Though apparently diverse, these approaches to "other knowledges" share the idea that people with different marginalized identities have different knowledges, stemming from their shared, embodied, and lived experiences as members of those identity groups, especially of systemic oppression. Such people are seen as disadvantaged, because they are forced to operate within a "dominant" system that is not their own. But they are also seen as enjoying unique advantages because of their familiarity with multiple epistemic systems. Thus, they can alternately be victims of "epistemic violence" when their knowledge is not included or recognized, or of "epistemic exploitation" when they are asked to share it.

These changes in approach have been steadily eroding the barrier between scholarship and activism. Working from a particular ideological standpoint used to be considered bad in teaching and scholarship. Teachers and scholars were expected to set aside their own biases and beliefs in order to approach subjects as objectively as possible. If they didn't, academics knew that other scholars could—and would—point out bias or motivated reasoning and counter it with evidence and argument. Teachers could consider themselves successful if their students didn't know their political or ideological positions.

This isn't how Critical Social Justice scholarship and education works. Teaching is now supposed to be a political act, and only one type of politics is acceptable—identity politics, as defined by Critical Social Justice and Theory. (Note: The term "identity politics" is often said to be relevant to the Civil Rights Movement of the 1950s and 1960s, but its first usage was in 1977 from a group of radical Critical Theorists, so it technically means something more specific to the Critical Theory approach.) In subjects ranging from gender studies to English literature, it's now perfectly acceptable to state a theoretical or ideological position and then use it to examine the material, without including any evidence or alternative explanations. Now, scholars can openly declare themselves to be activists and teach courses that require students to accept the ideologi-

cal basis of Critical Social Justice as true and produce work that
supports it.

One particularly infamous 2016 paper titled "Women's
Studies as Virus: Institutional Feminism, Affect, and the Projection of Danger" even *favorably* compared women's studies to
HIV, Ebola, and SARS (and cancer!), advocating that it spread
its version of feminism like an immune-suppressing virus,
using students-turned-activists as carriers, calling "the metaphor of the virus" an "ideal feminist" pedagogy or approach to
teaching. Scholars can, of course, be activists and activists can
be scholars, but combining these two roles can create problems. When a political stance is taught at university, it's likely
to become an orthodoxy that can't be questioned.

Applied postmodern ideas have escaped the boundaries of
the university in ways that the original postmodern Theory did
not, and they did so at least in part because of their ability to
be acted upon. Out in the world, these ideas have gained sway.
The postmodern knowledge and political principles are now
routinely evoked by activists and increasingly also by corporations, media, public figures, and the general public.

Everyday citizens are increasingly confused about what's
happened to society and how it happened so quickly. They hear
complaints about cultural appropriation and laments about
the lack of representation of certain identity groups in the arts.
They hear demands to "decolonize" everything from academic curricula to hairstyles to mathematics. They hear that only
white people can be racist and that they always are, by default.
Politicians, actors, and artists pride themselves on being inter-

sectional. Companies flaunt their respect for diversity, while firing employees who disagree with progressive politics. Organizations and activist groups of all kinds announce that they are inclusive, but only of people who agree with them. American engineers have been fired from corporations like Google for saying that gender differences exist, and British comedians have been sacked by the BBC for repeating jokes that could be seen as racist by Americans.

Applied postmodernism has come into its own, and it's being widely spread by activists. It's now an operational mythology for a wide swathe of society, especially on the left. It's very difficult to challenge a dominant orthodoxy.

Most people—let alone corporations, organizations, and public figures—aren't radical cultural constructivists. However, because these ideas offer the appearance of deep explanations to complicated problems, they've successfully morphed from obscure academic theories to part of the general "wisdom" about how the world works. These ideas are so widespread that matters won't improve until we show them for what they are and resist them—ideally by using consistent liberal principles and ethics.

Over the next five chapters, we'll explain how these applied Theories have developed. Then, in chapter 8, we'll explain how they came to be taken for granted as capital-T Truth.

3 POSTCOLONIAL THEORY
Deconstructing the West to Save the Other

Postcolonial Theory's goal is to deconstruct "the West"—a loose group of countries including the United States, the United Kingdom, Canada, Australia, France, Germany, and other Western European countries.

Unlike race and gender Theories, which had developed mature lines of thought before postmodernism took hold in cultural studies, postcolonial Theory came almost directly out of postmodern thought. Today, it also has a specific purpose: *decolonization*—the systematic undoing of colonialism in all its manifestations and impacts.

Not all postcolonial scholars are postmodern—many are materialists or Marxists, who study colonialism and its aftermath in terms of economics and politics—but the key figures were, and the postmodern approach dominates current postcolonial scholarship and activism.

Postcolonialism arose after the collapse of European colonialism, which had dominated global politics from the fif-
teenth century into the middle of the twentieth. This brand of
colonialism was based on the assumption that the European
powers had a right to expand their territories and exert their
political and cultural authority over other peoples and regions.

This sort of empire-building attitude was typical of many, if
not most, cultures before the twentieth century, but European
colonialism armed itself with potent metanarratives in order
to justify its domination. This included *la mission civilisatrice*
(the civilizing mission) in French colonialism—a religious rationale to justify the oppression of indigenous people—and,
in the North American context, Manifest Destiny—a widely
held belief in the 1800s that the United States was destined to
expand across the continent. These concepts were central to
moral philosophy and political organization from before the
Enlightenment right through the modern period.

European colonialism collapsed with surprising speed in
the twentieth century, especially following World War II. By
the early 1960s, both the academy and the general public had
moral concerns about colonialism, especially those on the left.
Postcolonial Theorists rejected colonial metanarratives and deconstructed colonialism's discourses (ways of speaking about
things), which sought to protect the so-called right of those
with power and privilege (read: "civilized" Western and Christian cultures) to dominate other cultures seen as "uncivilized"
and "barbaric."

Postcolonialism as an Applied Postmodern Project

In the mid-twentieth century, as concerns about colonialism grew, the work of psychiatrist Frantz Fanon rapidly gained influence. Fanon, who was born on the island of Martinique under French colonial rule, is considered foundational to postcolonial Theory. His 1952 book, *Black Skins, White Masks*, offers a powerful critique of both racism and colonialism. His 1959 work, *A Dying Colonialism*, chronicles the changes in culture and politics during Algeria's war of independence from France. That said, Fanon was extremely radical and openly advocated for insurrectionary violence throughout his work, which he considered fully justified.

His 1961 book, *The Wretched of the Earth*, set the stage for postcolonial Theory. To Fanon, colonialism was a systematic denial of the humanity of colonized people. Throughout his book, he describes what he sees as the literal erasure of people's identity and dignity. Colonized people, he insists, must violently resist this in order to maintain their mental health and self-respect. Fanon's book was both deeply critical and openly revolutionary—attitudes that have influenced postcolonialism and the more radical aspects of leftist activism ever since.

Writing in 1961, however, Fanon was hardly a postmodernist. His criticisms drew mainly on Lenin's Marxist critiques of capitalism, his analysis relied heavily on psychoanalytic theory, and his philosophy was essentially liberationist. (Note: "Liberationism" is a philosophical school that seeks liberation from "existing societies," including liberalism, which it believes are structurally oppressive, for other alternatives, particularly socialism and communism.) Later thinkers, including Edward Said, the father of postcolonial Theory, took inspiration from Fanon's depiction of the psychological impacts of having one's culture, language, and religion subordinated to another. Fanon argued that the colonialist *mind-set* has to be disrupted and, if possible, reversed by people who have been subjected to colonial rule. This focus on attitudes, biases, and discourses fits well with postmodernism.

Postcolonial Theorists also see their work as a project geared toward overcoming certain mind-sets baked into colonialism, rather than focusing on its practical and material effects. The key idea in postcolonial Theory is that the West constructs itself in opposition to the East, through the way it talks:

- "We're rational, they're superstitious."

- "We're honest, they're deceptive."

- "We're normal, they're exotic."

- "We're advanced, they're primitive."

- "We're liberal, they're barbaric."

The East is constructed as a foil for the West to compare itself to. The term *the other* or *othering* describes this denigration of other people in order to feel superior. Said called this mind-set "Orientialism"—a move that allowed him to attach a powerful pejorative to Orientalists, meaning those scholars and academics who studied the Far East, South Asia, and especially the Middle East from a Western perspective.

Said, a Palestinian-American Theorist, presented his new ideas in his book *Orientalism*, published in 1978. This book not only laid a foundation for the development of postcolonial Theory, but also brought the concept of applicable postmodern Theory to an American audience. Said drew primarily on Fanon and Foucault, especially Foucault's notions of "power/ knowledge." Although Said later had many criticisms of Foucault's approach, he considered power-knowledge instrumental to understanding Orientalism. He insisted that Orientalism "cannot possibly" be understood without Foucault's ideas.

This desire to deconstruct the West has dominated postcolonial Theory ever since. A lot of postcolonial scholarship involves reading Orientalism into texts. Said's project was a literary endeavor—in particular, he took issue with Joseph Conrad's 1899 novella *Heart of Darkness*, which raises significant questions about racism and colonialism. Rather than advocating a broad understanding of thematic elements of the text, Said preferred to scrutinize texts through "close reading," in order to uncover the various ways in which Western discourses uplift the superior West over the inferior East.

In Said's work, applied postmodern discourse analysis sees power imbalances in the interactions between dominant and marginalized cultural groups and reenvisions history from the perspective of the oppressed. Such an approach can be done productively, by recovering neglected voices and perspectives to give a fuller and more accurate picture of history, but it's often used to rewrite history in accordance with local or political narratives or to elevate multiple contradictory histories and then, in typical postmodern fashion, deny that any of them are objectively true.

In the introduction to *Orientalism,* we see the postmodern idea that knowledge is not found but made. Said writes,

> My argument is that history is made by men and women, just as it can also be unmade and rewritten, always with various silences and elisions, always with shapes imposed and disfigurements tolerated, so that "our" East, "our" Orient becomes "ours" to possess and direct.

This isn't just deconstruction—it's a call to reconstruct under an entirely new (and radical) system. Postcolonial Theory is thus the earliest activism-oriented category to arise within the *applied postmodern* school of thought.

Along with Said, two other scholars are foundational to postcolonial Theory: Gayatri Chakravorty Spivak and Homi K. Bhabha. Their work is thoroughly and explicitly postmodern, and because of their use of Jacques Derrida's deconstruction of language, it's obscure and very conceptually difficult. Spivak's most significant contribution to postcolonial Theory is probably her 1988 essay titled "Can the Subaltern Speak?," which focuses intensely on language and the role power structures play in constraining it.

Spivak argues that *subalterns*—colonized peoples of subordinate status—have no access to speech, even when they seem to be expressing themselves, because power has permeated discourse and created insurmountable barriers to communication for those who exist outside of the dominant discourses. In "Can the Subaltern Speak?" she drew upon Said and Foucault to develop the concept of *epistemic violence,* which describes the harm done to colonized people when their knowledge structures are marginalized by dominant discourses.

Spivak adopts this deconstructive idea from Derrida but argued that maintaining some group stereotypes can help cultivate solidarity among colonized people. She calls this "strategic essentialism." *Essentialism*, she tells us, is a linguistic tool of domination. Colonizers justify their oppression by regarding the subordinated group as a monolithic "other" that can be stereotyped and disparaged. *Strategic essentialism* applies this same sense of monolithic group identity as an act of resistance, deemphasizing diversity within the subordinated group for the purpose of promoting common goals through a common identity. It defines a particular kind of identity politics, built around intentional double standards.

Spivak takes more inspiration from Derrida than from Said and Foucault. Because of Derrida's focus on the ambiguity and fluidity of language, Spivak's work is deeply ambiguous and obscure. For example, she writes,

> Derrida marks radical critique with the danger of appropriating the other by assimilation. He reads catachresis at the origin. He calls for a rewriting of the utopian structural impulse as "rendering delirious that interior voice that is the voice of the other in us."

Impractical and impenetrable language was the fashion at the time for Theorists, especially among postcolonial Theorists. Bhabha, who held sway over the field through the 1990s, is even worse than Spivak in his ability to produce nearly incomprehensible writing. Bhabha focuses mainly on the role language plays in constructing knowledge, and his writing is notoriously difficult to read.

In 1998, he won second place in *Philosophy and Literature*'s Bad Writing Contest—beaten only by feminist Judith Butler—for the sentence,

> If, for a while, the ruse of desire is calculable for the uses of discipline, soon the repetition of guilt, justification, pseudo-scientific theories, superstition, spurious authorities, and classifications can be seen as the desperate effort to "normalize" formally the disturbance of a discourse of splitting that violates the rational, enlightened claims of its enunciatory modality.

Broken down, this wacky sentence, in context, says that racist, sexual jokes are told by colonizers initially to control a subordinate group, but that, ultimately, they are attempts by colonizers to convince themselves that their own ways of talking about things make sense because they are secretly terrified they don't.

Bhabha's work is criticized for being unnecessarily complicated and difficult to put to use in addressing postcolonial issues. He also most explicitly rejects the materialist, political (mostly Marxist) approach to postcolonial studies—the approach that would look at the economic and material impacts of colonialism on real people and how their well-being is affected. Bhabha even finds the language of the postmodern Theory he uses potentially problematic, asking, "Is the language of theory merely another power ploy of the culturally privileged Western élite to produce a discourse of the Other that reinforces its own power-knowledge equation?"

This postmodern focus has consequences. Such an investigation isn't concerned with the material realities affecting countries and people that were previously under colonial power—it's an analysis of attitudes, beliefs, speech, and mind-sets, which are sacralized or problematized. Theorists construct these simplistically from assumptions that position white Westerners (and knowledge thought of as "white" and "Western," like modern medicine) as superior to Eastern, black, and brown people (and "knowledges" associated with non-Western cultures, like traditional medicine), despite that being precisely the stereotype they claim to want to fight.

Mind-Sets Compared

Of course, colonialist narratives existed. Consider this repulsive, tough-to-read passage from 1871:

> Nature has made a race of workers, the Chinese race, who have wonderful manual dexterity, and almost no sense of honour; govern them with justice, levying from them, in return for the blessing of such a government, an ample allowance for the conquering race, and they will be satisfied; a race of tillers of the soil, the Negro; treat him with kindness and humanity, and all will be as it should; a race of masters

and soldiers, the European race. . . . Let each do what he is made for, and all will be well.

Thankfully, we don't see this attitude much today. It gradually became less and less morally acceptable over the twentieth century, with the fall of colonialism and rise of the civil rights movements, and would now rightly be seen as far-right extremism. Nevertheless, postcolonial Theory refers to these attitudes as if their past existence still influences the way people discuss and view issues today. Postcolonial Theory holds that permanent problems have been handed down to us through language constructed centuries ago.

The social changes that made that passage so repulsive for us today weren't based on postmodern Theory. They came before it, out of universal and individual liberalism. Liberalism holds that science, reason, and human rights belong to everyone, not to any one set of people, whether they be men or white Westerners or anyone else. Postmodern postcolonialism differs radically from this liberal approach and is often criticized for helping to prop up Orientalist binaries, rather than seeking to overcome them.

A Western colonial mind-set says: *"Westerners are rational and scientific while Asians are irrational and superstitious. Therefore, Europeans must rule Asia for its own good."*

A liberal mind-set says: *"All humans have the capacity to be rational and scientific. Therefore, all humans must have all opportunities and freedoms."*

A postmodern mind-set says: *"The West has decided that rationality and science are good in order to perpetuate its own power and marginalize nonrational, nonscientific forms of knowledge production from elsewhere."*

The liberal mind-set rejects colonialism's arrogant claim that reason and science belong to white Westerners. The postmodern one accepts colonialism's claim but regards reason and science themselves as oppressive—an oppression they try to correct by applying the core tenets of postmodernism. The applied postmodern mind-set on colonialism is similar to the postmodern one, but adds an activist component, sometimes called "radical egalitarianism," from Critical Theory.

An applied postmodern mind-set says: *"The West has decided that rationality and science are good in order to perpetuate its own power and marginalize nonrational, nonscientific forms of knowledge production from else-where. Therefore, we must now devalue white, Western ways of knowing because they belong to white Westerners and promote Eastern ones in order to equalize the power imbalance."*

This practice is frequently referred to as *decolonizing* and leads to seeking *research justice*.

Decolonize Everything

Initially, postcolonial scholarship mostly took the form of literary criticism, analyzing writing about colonialism, and was frequently written in highly obscure postmodern Theoretical prose. As the field expanded, it simplified. By the early 2000s, the concept of *decolonizing* things started dominating scholarship and activism. New scholars also began to use and develop the concepts in different ways. They retained the two postmodern principles and the four themes, but expanded their focus beyond ideas and speech about literal colonialism to include perceived attitudes toward people of certain identity statuses. These included displaced indigenous groups and people from racial or ethnic minorities—people who could be considered subaltern or diasporic (people who have spread beyond or been dispelled from their homeland), or whose non-Western beliefs, cultures, or customs have been devalued. Today, the goals of postcolonial Theory have become more concrete: focusing less on disrupting colonialist discourses and more on taking active steps to decolonize.

"Decolonizing" something that isn't literally colonized can mean different things. It can refer to efforts to include more scholars of all nationalities and races, as seen in recent campaigns by the United Kingdom's National Union of Students (NUS): "Why Is My Curriculum White?" (2015) and #LiberateMyDegree (2016). However, it can also refer to a drive for a diversity of "knowledges" and epistemologies under Theory, such as tribal superstitions and witchcraft, often described as "other ways of knowing," as well as a drive to critique, problematize, and disparage so-called Western knowledge.

This sometimes takes the form of treating physical spaces like a "text" in need of deconstruction. A good example is the

2015 Rhodes Must Fall movement, which began at South Africa's University of Cape Town in 2015 as an effort to remove a statue commemorating British businessman and politician Cecil Rhodes. Rhodes was responsible for much of the legal framework of apartheid, South Africa's system of institutionalized racial segregation that lasted into the 1990s. It's perfectly reasonable to object to favorable depictions of him, but the movement spread to universities around the world and grew far beyond just objecting to the exploitative and illiberal practices of apartheid and colonialism. At the University of Oxford, for instance, demands for symbolic changes, such as the removal of colonialist statues and imagery, were wrapped up with other activist demands, including a push to increase representation of ethnic and racial minorities (who agree with Theory) on campus and to increase focus on *what* was studied in the curriculum and *how* it was being studied.

In the introduction to an anthology of essays called *Decolonising the University* published in 2018, editors Gurminder K. Bhambra, Dalia Gebrial, and Kerem Nişancıoğlu explain that decolonization can refer to the study of colonialism's material manifestations and discourses, but that it can also offer *alternative ways of thinking*. This is an example of *standpoint theory* (or *positional knowledge*)—the belief that knowledge comes from the lived experience of different identity groups, who are differently positioned in society and see different aspects of it.

For decolonial scholars, both "Eurocentric forms of knowledge" and the authority we (unjustly, in their view) grant to Western universities are problems, and "the point is not simply to deconstruct such understandings, but to transform them." In other words, by using activism to achieve a symbolic aim (e.g., removing statues on campus), decolonization activists are also attempting to reform education so that it will rely more explicitly on their applications of Theory.

Decolonization efforts have two focal points: national origin and race. Bhambra and crew, influenced by Said, see knowledge as related to geography: "The content of university knowledge remains principally governed by the West for the West." Theorist Kehinde Andrews is more heavily influenced by critical race Theory and sees knowledge as closely related to race: "The neglect of Black knowledge by society is no accident but a direct result of racism." We must, Andrews says, "forever leave behind the idea that knowledge can be produced value free. Our politics shape our understanding of the world and the pretence of neutrality ironically makes our endeavours less valid."

Note where he says that "value free" (bias-free) and "neutral" knowledge is impossible to obtain and that we should forever abandon trying to obtain it. This is the postmodern knowledge principle in action. Theory holds that the knowledge that's currently most valued is intrinsically white and Western, and it interprets this as an injustice—no matter how reliably that knowledge was produced. This is the postmodern political principle. This also shows up in the "Aims" of the Rhodes Must Fall movement at Oxford, which sought to "remedy the highly selective narrative of traditional academia—which frames the West as sole producers of universal knowledge—by integrating subjugated and local epistemologies . . . [and creating] a more intellectually rigorous, complete academy."

What they're talking about is devaluing knowledge if it was discovered in the West, and uplifting other knowledge—even if it doesn't accurately describe reality—just because it came out of colonized places. This leads to a belief that rigor and accuracy come not from good methodology, skepticism, and evidence, but from the identity of those who produce it. This approach doesn't tend to produce useful new knowledge, but that's considered unimportant—at least it's more *just*.

This view is used to advocate and engage in historical revisionism—rewriting history, often in the service of a political agenda—by accusing rigorous research methods of being "positivist" (a philosophy that says that only things that can be scientifically verified can be true) and thus biased. As Dalia Gebrial puts it in *Decolonising the University*:

> The public's sense of what history is remains influenced by positivist tendencies, whereby the role of the historian is to simply "reveal" facts about pasts that are worth revealing, in a process removed from power. This epistemological insistence on history as a positivist endeavour functions as a useful tool of coloniality in the institution, as it effaces the power relations that underpin what the "production of history" has thus far looked like.

The complaint here is that history can't be trusted because it's "written by the winners." There's some truth to that, but good historians try to eliminate their own bias from their work as much as possible by seeking disconfirming evidence of their claims. The decolonization approach tends to fail to take this into account, leading its interpretations into excessive cynicism.

For example, medieval war historians often advise readers to divide the number of soldiers claimed to have fought in a battle by ten to get a more realistic number. This tendency to massively overstate numbers (probably to make the story more exciting) was discovered by historians researching records of soldiers' pay. Similarly, feminist scholars have used legal and financial records to reveal that women have played a much more active role in society, law, and business than we once thought. Our knowledge of history is skewed by the biased records that survive, but the way to mitigate this is to investigate the evidence and reveal the bias of common narratives, not to include a greater range of biases and declare some of them immune to criticism.

In addition to criticizing evidence-based scholarship, decolonial narratives attack rationality, which postcolonial scholars see as a Western way of thinking. For example, the essay "Decolonising Philosophy," which appears in *Decolonising the University*, begins,

> it will be difficult to contest the idea that, generally speaking, philosophy as a field or a discipline in modern Western universities remains a bastion of Eurocentrism, whiteness in general, and white heteronormative male structural privilege and superiority in particular.

In the typical style of standpoint theory, the essay's authors think philosophical concepts are worth only as much as their authors' gender, race, sexuality, and geography. Ironically, the authors are using Foucault's idea of "power/knowledge," despite Foucault being a white Western man.

Foucault's concept of knowledge and the ways it's used to deconstruct categories we accept as real influences this line of Theoretical thought. For example, you see it in this description of decolonization's mission, from "Decolonising Philosophy":

> Any serious effort to decolonise philosophy cannot be satisfied with simply adding new areas to an existing arrangement of power/knowledge, leaving the Eurocentric norms that define the field as a whole in place, or reproducing such norms themselves. For example, when engaging in non-European philosophies it is important to avoid reproducing problematic conceptions of time, space and subjectivity that are embedded in the Eurocentric definition of European philosophy and its many avatars.

In other words, it's not enough to just add other philosophical approaches to the field one wishes to decolonize. European philosophy must be entirely rejected—even to the point of deconstructing *time and space* as Western constructs.

You see all four of the postmodern themes in postcolonial Theory—the blurring of boundaries, the power of language, cultural relativism, and the loss of the universal and individual in favor of group identity. These themes are central to the postcolonial Theory mind-set and decolonize movement. Relegating time, space, and reason to the status of "Western construct" is a textbook example of applied, actionable postmodernism. The action it advocates is often referred to as "research justice."

Achieving Research Justice

Research justice refers to a belief that science, reason, empiricism, objectivity, universality, and subjectivity are overrated ways of obtaining knowledge, while emotion, experience, traditional narratives and customs, and spiritual beliefs are undervalued. Proponents of research justice say fair, more complete systems of knowledge production would value the latter at least as much as the former—or more, because science and reason have dominated for so long.

The 2015 book *Research Justice: Methodologies for Social Change*, edited by Andrew Jolivette, is a key text here. Jolivette, a professor and former department chair of American Indian Studies at San Francisco State University, explains the aims of this method in his introduction:

> "[R]esearch justice" is a strategic framework and methodological intervention that aims to transform structural inequalities in research. . . . It is built around a vision of equal political power and legitimacy for different forms of knowledge, including the cultural, spiritual, and experiential, with the goal of greater equality in public policies and laws that rely on data and research to produce social change.

This is activism aiming to revolutionize understandings of knowledge and rigor in universities and to influence government policies away from evidenced and reasoned work and toward the emotional, religious, cultural, and traditional, with an emphasis on *lived experience.*

This comes across strongly in the 2004 book *Decolonizing Research in Cross-Cultural Contexts: Critical Personal Narratives,* which focuses on indigenous studies. Citing Homi K. Bhabha, the editors introduce the essays by claiming,

> These works stand at the center of the "beginning of the presencing" of a disharmonious, restive, unharnessable (hence unessentializable) knowledge that is produced at the ex-centric site of neo/post/colonial resistance, "which can never allow the national (*read: colonial/Western*) history to look itself narcissistically in the eye."

This means that the authors of the essays in this volume don't have to make sense, produce reasoned arguments, avoid logical contradiction, or provide any evidence for their claims. The normal expectations of scholarly "research" don't apply when pursuing research justice. This is obviously alarming.

As Linda Tuhiwai Smith, a professor of indigenous education at the University of Waikato in New Zealand, explains:

> [F]rom the vantage point of the colonised, a position from which I write and choose to privilege, the term "research" is inextricably linked to European imperialism and colonialism. The word itself "research" is probably one of the dirtiest words in the indigenous world's vocabulary.

It's unclear how this attitude will help people in the "indigenous world," which needs evidence-based research just as much as the rest of us in the twenty-first century.

"Research justice" judges scholarly work by the identity of its producer, not by its quality, and gives preference to work postcolonial Theory sees as marginalized. This is an understandable move for postmodernists, who deny that there can be any objective criteria of quality. But in the sciences (including social science), there is an objective measurement of quality: reality. Some scientific theories work, and others don't. Good scientists and scholars ask questions, develop hypotheses, conduct experiments and studies that properly test their hypotheses, and draw conclusions by studying the data. They don't forgo evidence-based research or start with their conclusions.

Scientific theories that don't correspond with reality can't benefit marginalized people, or anyone.

Maintaining the Problem, Backward

The attitude that evidence-based research and reasoned arguments belong to the West while experience-based and irrational "knowledge" belongs to colonized or displaced indigenous people is, of course, not universally accepted by colonized and indigenous scholars. Many of them produce solid work on economic, political, and legal issues, and they criticize the postmodern approach to postcolonialism.

One of the most outstanding critics of this Theory-based approach is the Indian postcolonial scholar Meera Nanda. She argues that, by assigning science and reason to the West and traditional, spiritual, experiential beliefs to India, postmodern scholars perpetuate Orientalism and make it harder to address the many real issues that can best be tackled using science and reason. Nanda observes that, in these critics' view, "modern science is as much a local tradition of the West, as the indigenous knowledge of the non-Western subaltern is a local knowledge of his culture."

The Theoretical approach to postcolonialism just reverses the power structures. While colonialism constructs the East as a foil to the West, postcolonial Theory intentionally constructs the East as noble, oppressed opposition to the West (while liberalism says that people are people, wherever they live). For Nanda, this postmodern approach harms the technological and social progress that would benefit the poorer people of India and gives power to conservative attitudes about progress:

> Postmodern/post-colonial theory's animus against the Enlightenment values and its indulgence towards the contradictions make it eminently compatible with a typically right-wing resolution of the asynchronicity (or the time-lag) between advanced technology and a backward social context that developing societies typically experience in the process of modernization.

Furthermore, Nanda believes it's demeaning to Indian people to say that their knowledge is irrational and superstitious and to assume that science is a tradition that belongs to the West, rather than a uniquely human development that is extremely beneficial to all societies.

This is what we believe, too.

A Dangerous, Patronizing Theory

Postcolonial Theory poses a real-world threat to society that the original postmodernism did not. The drives to tear down paintings, smash statues, and rewrite history are particularly alarming. When Winston Churchill, Joseph Conrad, and Rudyard Kipling become nothing more than symbols of racist imperialism and their achievements and writings are too tainted to be acknowledged, we lose the potential for nuanced discussion of history and progress, as well as the positive contributions of the men themselves.

Worse still, postcolonial Theory and the way it disparages science and reason threaten the foundations of advanced contemporary societies and slows the progress of developing ones. Many developing countries would benefit from upgraded technology, which could improve some of the world's most significant causes of human suffering: malaria, water shortages, and poor sanitation in remote rural areas. Depriving developing countries of the fruits of modern science because it comes from oppressive "Western" knowledge wouldn't just be patronizing—it would also be negligent and dangerous.

Postcolonialism's cultural relativism also does harm. It says that because the West has trampled on other cultures and enforced alien moral frameworks on them, it must now stop criticizing any aspect of those cultures, and in some cases, stop helping them in any way.

For example, feminists from Saudi Arabia, secular liberals from Pakistan, and LGBT-rights activists from Uganda have used hashtags in English on social media to draw the attention of the English-speaking world to human rights abuses in their countries. These campaigns have received little response from applied postmodern scholars and activists who should support these causes. They have two common arguments to justify themselves.

First, they argue that getting a non-Western culture to accept that there are human rights abuses taking place locally requires colonizing that culture with Western ideas about human rights. This is forbidden, because it reinforces the power dynamic that postcolonial Theory wants to dismantle.

Second, postcolonial Theory frequently claims that any human rights abuses occurring in previously colonized countries are the legacy of colonialism. This often isn't true. Some human rights abuses can be connected to non-Western religious and cultural beliefs—for example, the widespread abuse of women, secularists, and LGBT people in countries controlled by strict Islamists. Postcolonial Theory doesn't take their strict socially conservative views as a feature of authoritarian interpretations of Islam—as the Islamists themselves claim—but instead sees them as a result of Western colonialism and imperialism, which postcolonial Theory says perverted that culture and caused it to become abusive. This often prevents secular activist campaigns that could help solve those problems.

Because postcolonial Theory views knowledge and ethics as cultural constructs maintained by language, people who believe in postcolonial Theory can be really hard to have discussions with. They see evidenced and reasoned arguments as

Western constructs, and therefore invalid or even oppressive. People who disagree with them are seen as defending racist, colonialist, or imperialist attitudes. The postcolonial mind-set can't help but hear examples of "othering," "Orientalism," and "appropriation" in everything.

This problem shouldn't be underestimated. We can only learn from the realities of colonialism and its aftermath by studying them rigorously. Those postcolonial scholars and activists who deny the existence of objective reality and want to rewrite history aren't doing this. Neither are those who reject logical reasoning, evidence-based research, science, and medicine, those who argue that space and time themselves are Western constructs, nor those who write incomprehensibly complicated prose and deny that language can have meaning anyway.

These scholars generally work in elite Western universities, operating under a dense theoretical framework. Their work is of very little practical value to people in formerly colonized countries, who are busy trying to live and deal with the political and economic aftermath of colonialism. They probably wouldn't have any use for an ideology arguing that math is a weapon of Western imperialism, that sees alphabetical literacy as colonial technology and postcolonial appropriation, or that confronts France and the United States about their cultural appropriation and devaluation of twerking—and yes, each of these arguments has actually been made by scholars working in postcolonial Theory.

4 QUEER THEORY
Freeing Gender and Sexuality from the Normal

Queer Theory is about freedom from the normal, especially when it comes to gender and sexuality. It says that oppression happens every time language constructs a sense of what is "normal" by defining categories—such as sex (male and female), gender (masculine and feminine), sexuality (straight, gay, lesbian, bisexual, and so on)—and slotting people into them. These seemingly straightforward concepts are seen as oppressive, if not violent, and so the main objective of queer Theory is to examine, question, and subvert them in order to break them down.

To do this, queer Theory uses the postmodern knowledge principle—which rejects the possibility that an objective reality is attainable—and the postmodern political principle—which sees society as structured in unjust systems of power. Queer Theory's ultimate purpose is to identify the ways linguistic categories create oppression, and to disrupt them. It also uses the postmodern themes of the power of language (language creates the categories, enforces them, and scripts people into them) and the blurring of boundaries (the boundaries are arbitrary and oppressive, and can be erased by blurring them).

Queer Theory values incoherence, illogic, and unintelligibility as tools to flout the norm in favor of the "queer," which it proudly calls an "identity without an essence." It's vague by design and largely irrelevant in the real world except through social erosion, but it has profoundly influenced the development of postmodern Theory into its more recent applied forms, such as gender studies, trans activism, disability studies, and fat studies.

A Brief History of Queer Theory

Like postcolonial Theory, queer Theory developed in response to a particular historical context. It grew out of the radical groups that had been revolutionizing feminist, gay, and lesbian studies, and their activism since the 1960s. The gay rights movement also helped spark a new interest in the study of homosexuality, and the ways it had been categorized and stigmatized, both historically and in the present. Queer Theory was also deeply influenced by the AIDS crisis of the 1980s, which made gay rights an urgent social and political issue.

Like postcolonial Theory, queer Theory has a solid underlying point. The way we see sexuality *has* changed. Throughout Christian history, male homosexuality has been considered a terrible sin. In stark contrast, in ancient Greek culture, it was acceptable for men to have sex with adolescent boys until they were ready to marry—at which point it was expected that they would switch to having sex with women. In both cases, homosexuality was viewed as *something that people did* rather than *who they were.*

The idea that one could *be* gay only began to gain recognition in the 1800s, appearing first in medical texts and homosexual subcultures. Public perception of homosexuals then gradually shifted as sexology became an active area of study in the late 1800s. By the middle of the twentieth century, gay people were seen less as degenerate criminals who should be punished and more as shamefully disordered individuals who required psychiatric treatment. Still awful, but believe it or not, this was actually a slight improvement. Over the second half of the twentieth century, this attitude shifted again until the liberal attitude toward homosexuality gained the moral high ground. This attitude is best summed up as "It's okay to be gay."

However, this universal liberal idea, which emphasizes our common humanity, is considered problematic by queer Theorists. It presents sexual orientations as stable categories, not fluid labels people can move between whenever they like. It doesn't define LGBT statuses as social constructs, built by the powerful in the service of dominance and oppression, but as something that a person just *is,* due to some combination of nature and nurture. For queer Theory, then, rather surprisingly, it can be considered *not* "okay to be gay," because if it were okay, that would make being gay another kind of *nor-*

mal, which queer Theory resists on principle. This is why many gay rights activists of the 1990s had to fight their rights battle on two fronts: one against the social conservatives who saw homosexuality as sinful and wrong and the other against the queer Theorists who wanted to prevent the normalization (that is, full acceptance) of homosexuality so they could keep it a site for radical, deconstructive identity politics.

While there have been dramatic changes in how we view homosexuality over the last century and a half, our understanding of sex and gender hasn't changed very much. We've generally always understood that our species has two sexes, with most peoples' gender—the outward expression of their sex—being aligned with their sex. Gender *roles*, however, have changed considerably. Throughout most of Christian history, men were associated with the public sphere and the mind and women with the private sphere and the body. Because of their respective reproductive functions, women were considered biologically better suited to subservient, domestic, and nurturing roles and men to leadership, public engagement, and assertive managerial roles. This attitude is called *biological essentialism*, and it dominated society until roughly the end of the 1800s, when feminist thought and activism began to chip away at it.

As biological essentialism fell by the wayside, we needed another way to distinguish between sex and gender. The word "gender" wasn't used to describe humans until the twentieth century—some languages still have no comparable word—but it seems we've always had the *idea* of gender, and that we've always seen it as related to sex, but not synonymous. If the sentence, "She is a very masculine woman," makes sense to you, you already distinguish sex—a biological category—from gender—behaviors and traits that manifest more commonly but not exclusively in one sex and in varying degrees. History is full of examples of people referring to "manly" and "womanly," or masculine and feminine, traits and behaviors and applying these adjectives to both men and women in approving and disapproving ways.

A few big changes took place in the West in the latter half of the twentieth century due to a second wave of feminist activism, which followed an earlier wave of important feminist activism that began in the nineteenth century. While women won the right to vote in what is now referred to as the first wave of feminism, women gained control over their reproductive function and the right to work any job and be paid the same as men for the same work in this second wave. Today, women work in all professions and experience few legal or cultural barriers in the West, although they still don't make the same career choices in the same numbers as men do.

Similar changes came out of the gay rights movement, and eventually the Pride and trans rights movements, which have succeeded at removing many legal and cultural barriers for LGBT people. Most of these changes resulted from recognizing the biological roots of sex, gender, and sexuality, and realizing that people don't choose these elements of themselves. But queer Theorists, especially those with a feminist perspective, take this progress as evidence of the social construction of gender and sexuality. The gap between sex and gender has been taken as evidence that gender—and even sex—are made-up.

Like postcolonial Theorists, queer Theorists are less concerned with material progress than with how dominant discourses create and enforce categories like "male," "feminine," and "gay." The founders of queer Theory, including Gayle Rubin, Judith Butler, and Eve Kosofsky Sedgwick, drew significantly upon the work of Michel Foucault and his concept of *biopower*—the power of scientific (biological) discourses. Unfortunately, they don't realize that understanding sex, gender, and sexuality statuses as underlain by biology tends to lead people to become more accepting of differences, not less, because then sexual orientation and gender identity are seen as something individuals can't control, and therefore are not moral issues. Just as we don't blame a woman for being of a height more common to men, we shouldn't blame her for being attracted to women, which is more common to men. Liberalism generated the type of progress postmodern Theories often claim credit for, without using postmodern Theories.

To Queer, Verb; The Queer, Noun

Queer Theory is all about problematizing discourses (finding problematic issues in how we speak about things), deconstructing categories, and being profoundly skeptical of science. Following Foucault, it examines history and points out that categories and discourses that were accepted as true in the past aren't accepted anymore. This is used to argue that the categories that seem so obvious to us now—male/female, masculine/feminine, heterosexual/homosexual—are just socially constructed by the dominant discourses of today.

This, to the queer Theorist, doesn't just mean that we'll categorize sex, gender, and sexuality differently in the future, but also that we may soon consider such categories arbitrary and nearly infinitely flexible. This also follows Foucault, specifically his hope to expand the "potentialities of being" through his style of critique.

This is where the word *queer* comes in. "Queer" refers to anything that falls outside binaries (such as male/female, masculine/feminine, and heterosexual/homosexual), and it's also a way of challenging the links between sex, gender, and sexuality. For example, it questions expectations that women will be feminine and sexually attracted to men, and disputes that people must fall into any one category of male or female, masculine or feminine, or any particular sexuality. To be queer allows someone to be simultaneously male, female, or neither, to present as masculine, feminine, gender neutral, or any mixture of the three, and to adopt any sexuality—and to change any of these identities at any time.

This isn't just championing individual expression. It's a political statement about the socially constructed "realities" of sex, gender, and sexuality. Like the other postmodern Theories, queer Theory is a political project. Its political agenda is to challenge *normativity*—the idea that because some things are more common or regular to the human condition, they are the natural way for things to be.

Normativity is considered a bad thing by queer Theorists because they believe that if we consider something to be normal or natural, we consider it to be good. Thus, they often use prefixes like *hetero-* (straight), *cis-* (gender and sex match), and *thin-* (not obese) as pejoratives. By challenging normativity, queer Theory seeks to unite the minority groups who fall outside of normative categories under a single banner: "queer." This is supposed to be liberating for people who don't fall neatly into sex, gender, and sexuality categories, along with those who wouldn't if they hadn't been socialized into them. It produces a kind of coalition of minority gender and sexual identities.

In recent years it has become common to hear "queer" used as a verb, as well. Queering is about undoing norms to liberate people from the expectations that norms carry—for example, the expectation that women be "womanly" and men be "manly." Queering gender would mean treating the two most common categories, man and woman, as just as fluid and undefinable as the nonbinary space in between, and believing there would be as many nonbinary people as there are men or women if we were not socialized into believing differently— maybe even more!

Queer Theory believes that categorizing gender and sexuality (or anything else) enables normativity and uses it to constrain individuals. It addresses this problem in postmodern ways, which draw especially upon the work of Michel Foucault and Jacques Derrida. Their influence makes queer Theory notoriously difficult to define, because of its radical distrust of language and desire to avoid all categorization, including of itself. David Halperin attempts to define "queer" in his 1997 book, *Saint Foucault: Towards a Gay Hagiography*, describing it as "*whatever* is at odds with the normal, the legitimate, the dominant. *There is nothing in particular to which it necessarily refers. It is an identity without an essence.*"

Queer Theory also resists functional definitions of what it does. Papers that use queer Theory usually begin by examining an idea, problematizing it in "queering" (or "genderfucking"— an actual academic term!) ways, and eventually concluding that there can be no conclusions. As Annamarie Jagose, the author of *Queer Theory: An Introduction*, puts it, "It is not simply that queer has yet to solidify and take on a more consistent profile, but rather that its definitional indeterminacy, its elasticity, is one of its constituent characteristics."

The incoherence of queer Theory is a feature, not a bug.

The Queer Legacy of *The History of Sexuality*

As most people now acknowledge, many of our ideas about sex, gender, and sexuality—and particularly about their associated roles—are malleable. Nearly everyone now accepts that a combination of human biology and culture comes together to create expressions of sex, gender, and sexuality. As evolutionary biologist E. O. Wilson states, "No serious scholar would think that human behavior is controlled the way animal instinct is, without the intervention of culture."

Queer Theory takes a radically skeptical stance toward science. If biology makes an appearance in queer Theory–based scholarship, it's usually for one of two purposes: to problematize biology as a supremacist way of knowing that props up powerful groups, such as straight cisgender men; or to bring up the existence of intersex people, which no one denies. Intersex people are only pointed out to obscure the fact that an overwhelming proportion of *Homo sapiens* are either male- or female-sexed and their gender expression generally pairs with their sex. These facts are dismissed for supporting normativity.

Casting aside biology limits queer Theory's ability to actually investigate the way gender presentation and expectations are socialized into us, while making its potentially valuable insights almost irrelevant to those seriously studying these questions. There are biologists and psychologists advancing our knowledge of how the sexes differ (or don't) biologically and psychologically on average, how sexuality works, and why some people are gay, lesbian, bisexual, or transgender, but their work isn't welcome in queer Theory. It's looked at with suspicion, as a dangerous or even "violent" way to categorize and constrain everyone who doesn't fit neatly into one of two categories: "masculine man attracted to women" and "feminine woman attracted to men."

Michel Foucault is largely responsible for this understanding of the oppressive role of science. As well as "power/knowledge," he was concerned with "biopower"—how science legitimizes the knowledge that the powerful use to stay in power. In his four-volume study *The History of Sexuality*, Foucault argues that since the late 1600s, there has been an explosion of talk about sex—both the act and the biological concept. As scientists began to study and categorize sexuality, Foucault claims, they simultaneously constructed it and created the sexual identities and categories that we use today. He says:

The society that emerged in the nineteenth century—bourgeois, capitalist, or industrial society, call it what you will—did not confront sex with a fundamental refusal of recognition. On the contrary, it put into operation an entire machinery for producing true discourses concerning it.

Foucault's view was that the discourses this "machinery" produced became recognized as "truth" and then permeated all levels of society. This is a process of power but not, as Marxist philosophers had claimed, one in which religious or secular authorities enforce an ideology on the common people. In Marxist thought, power is like a weight, pressed down on the proletariat (the workers) from above by the bourgeoisie (the business owners). Foucault's (and Theory's) view is that power is a system we all constantly participate in by how we talk about things and what ideas we consider true. It's a system we're socialized into. In Foucault's view, science legitimizes knowledge—and therefore power—and it holds prestige in society because of its ability to do this.

Foucault called this "biopower," claiming that scientific discourse "set itself up as the supreme authority in matters of hygienic necessity," and "in the name of biological and historical urgency, it justified the racisms of the state" because it "grounded them in 'truth.'" Foucault argues that power runs through the whole system of society, perpetuating itself through discourses. He called this the "omnipresence of power." "Power is everywhere," Foucault writes, "not because it embraced everything, but because it comes from everywhere."

From these basic premises, first spelled out in the 1970s,

Foucault provided the philosophical foundations for the queer Theory of the 1990s.

The Fairy Godmothers of Queer Theory

Queer Theory evolved out of a postmodern view of sex, gender, and sexuality. Its three founding figures were Gayle Rubin, Judith Butler, and Eve Kosofsky Sedgwick, and they drew heavily upon Foucault to lay the cornerstones of queer Theory in the mid-1980s.

In her essay "Thinking Sex," first published in 1984, Gayle Rubin argues that what we consider morally "good sex" and morally "bad sex" are socially constructed by various groups and their discourses about sexuality. Rubin was deeply skeptical of biological studies of sex and sexuality. Her essay rejected what she saw as "sexual essentialism"—"the idea that sex is a natural force that exists prior to social life and shapes institutions." For Rubin,

> It is impossible to think with any clarity about the politics of race or gender as long as these are thought of as biological entities rather than as social constructs. Similarly, sexuality is impervious to political analysis as long as it is primarily conceived as a biological phenomenon or an aspect of individual psychology.

Rubin says we should believe sex, gender, and sexuality are social constructs *not* because it's necessarily true, but because it's *easier to politicize them and demand change* if they are social constructs than if they are biological. If discourses enforce the idea that they're biological, then they're more resistant to political activism.

This agenda-driven view goes against both the rigor of scientific inquiry and the ethics of universal liberal activism for gender and LGBT equality. Liberalism doesn't require us to believe that gender and sexuality are socially constructed in order to argue that discrimination is wrong.

Rubin states her position on this in "Thinking Sex":

> Concepts of sexual oppression have been lodged within that more biological understanding of sexuality. It is often easier to fall back on the notion of a natural libido subjected to inhumane repression than to reformulate concepts of sexual injustice within a more constructivist framework. But it is essential that we do so.

Rubin insists that it's crucial to reject biology and fully embrace the idea that sex and sexuality have been constructed in an unjust hierarchy, even though she recognizes that it would be easier to accept that different sexualities exist naturally and that some of them have been unfairly discriminated against. Dismissing biology was considered a political necessity, so we often see queer Theory rejecting science when its findings deviate from Theory, rejecting liberalism when it puts universal humanity first, and rejecting feminism when it regards women as a class of people oppressed by men. Instead, queer Theory prioritizes "queerness."

The most influential queer Theorist is Judith Butler. Her

work became influential in many forms of scholarship and even in wider society. Butler is an American philosopher influenced by French feminist thought who draws heavily upon postmodernism, especially the work of Foucault and Derrida. Butler's chief contribution to queer Theory was to question the links between sex (the biological categories of male and female), gender (the behaviors and traits commonly associated with one sex or the other), and sexuality (the nature of sexual desire).

In the 1990s, Butler argued that gender and sex are distinct, with no necessary association between the two. To support her theory, Butler employed her most well-known concept: *gender performativity*. This is a remarkably complicated idea defined in her 1993 book, *Bodies That Matter: On the Discursive Limits of "Sex."*

Although it sounds like it's referring to a stage performance, the concept of gender performativity doesn't refer to acting. A male actor could, for example, perform a female stage role while still knowing that he's a man. This isn't what Butler means when she describes gender as "performative." In her groundbreaking book *Gender Trouble: Feminism and the Subversion of Identity* (1990), Butler claims that gender roles are taught and learned—often unwittingly, through socialization—as sets of actions, behaviors, manners, and expectations, and that people perform those roles accordingly.

Gender, for Butler, is a set of things a person *does*, not who they *are*. Society enforces these actions and slots them into categories like "male" and "manly," so these roles become "real" through gender performativity. People learn to perform their gender "correctly" and end up perpetuating the social reality called "gender" because of immense social pressure. Butler's view is that people aren't born knowing that they're male, female, straight, or gay, so they don't act in accordance with any such innate factors. Instead, they're socialized into these roles from birth, then perpetuate and maintain the meaning in those roles by taking them up as performances that let them be identified as male, female, straight, or gay by other people (and themselves).

For Butler, the mission of queer Theory and activism is to liberate "the performative possibilities for proliferating gender configurations outside the restricting frames of masculinist domination and compulsory heterosexuality"—meaning that if we recognize gender as performative, we can see that it can be performed in ways that don't privilege the masculine and heterosexual.

Butler came to this conclusion by using Derrida's notion of *phallogocentrism*—the idea that the language that constructs reality privileges the masculine (and straight) over the feminine (and gay)—and by expanding upon Adrienne Rich's concept of *compulsory heterosexuality*—the idea that society sees heterosexuality as the natural state of being and homosexuality as a perversion, and forces people to comply by "doing straightness." Butler wasn't optimistic about our ability to destroy these dominant discourses: we can only trouble and disrupt them, to make space for those who don't fit.

As a solution, Butler proposed *the politics of parody,* a "subversive and parodic redeployment of power." This approach tries to turn the patterns of gender performativity upside down—particularly phallogocentrism and compulsory hetero-sexuality—by making fun of them. This is often achieved by "genderfucking," which *Wiktionary* defines as "the conscious effort to subvert traditional notions of gender identity and gender roles," through the employment of drag, say, or the "queer-camp" aesthetic, or generally (and ironically) by engaging in blatant performances that "bend gender."

The purpose of this parody is to make people aware of performativity and see it as the socially constructed, arbitrary, and oppressive illusion it is. The point is to achieve liberation from these categories and the expectations that come with them. If rigid categories of sex, gender, and sexuality can be made ridiculous, then they'll be less meaningful.

Butler went further than gender, though, and even called into question whether biological sex has any basis in reality at all. In *Gender Trouble*, she writes,

> If the immutable character of sex is contested, perhaps this construct called "sex" is as culturally constructed as gender; indeed, perhaps it was always already gender, with the consequence that the distinction between sex and gender turns out to be no distinction at all.

For her, the very existence of stable categories like "woman" leads to totalitarian and oppressive discourses. She describes the act of putting people into a category, such as a gender, that they feel does not adequately or accurately describe them as a kind of violence. For Butler, activism and scholarship must disrupt these discourses to minimize this "violence" of being categorized.

The focus on breaking down categories by acting as if they don't correspond to physical reality at all is also central to Eve Kosofsky Sedgwick's work. Her contributions to Theory are ultimately about resisting the temptation to solve contradictions, finding value in *plurality*—accepting many perspectives all at once, even when they contradict each other—and in *incoherence*—not attempting to make rational sense of anything. Consistent with the mind-set of applied postmodernism, she sees these values as useful for activism. She writes,

> In consonance with my emphasis on the performative relations of double and conflicted definition, the theorized prescription for a practical politics implicit in these readings is for a multi-pronged movement whose idealist and materialist impulses, whose minority-model and universalist-model strategies, and for that matter whose gender-separatist and gender-integrative analyses would likewise proceed in parallel without any high premium placed on ideological rationalization between them.

Here Sedgwick is saying that a productive movement could incorporate all the ideas found in LGBT scholarship and activism—even contradictory approaches—without needing to resolve ideological differences. She argues that the contradictions themselves can be politically valuable, partially because they would make the thinking behind the activism very difficult to understand and criticize. This is, of course, very queer.

These ideas are most prominent in Sedgwick's 1990 book,

The Epistemology of the Closet, which developed Foucault's idea that sexuality is a social construct made by scientific discourses—especially those created by medical authorities, who had classified homosexuality as a personality disorder. But Sedgwick reversed Foucault's belief that dominant discourses created homosexuality and heterosexuality. She argues that it's the binary of homosexuality and heterosexuality that gave us binary thinking—people are either gay *or* straight, male *or* female, masculine *or* feminine, instead of possibly being in between or both.

For Sedgwick, sexual binaries underlie all social binaries. She says that understanding the fluid complexities of sexuality is key to undoing many forms of black-and-white thinking in society. Her symbolism of the closet is based on this idea of false binaries: you're never fully in or out of the closet. The closet, to Sedgwick, symbolizes occupying contradictory realities at the same time, even in areas not related to sexuality. Embracing this is core to her approach to queer Theory, and in this we see the beginnings of the expansion of the queer to matters outside of sexuality, along with the use of "queer" as a verb.

Because she took a postmodernist approach, Sedgwick identified language—specifically, "speech acts"—as the way in which these unjust binaries and "the closet" are constructed and maintained. She saw her Theoretical approach as a liberatory revelation. She remarks,

> An assumption underlying the book is that the relations of
> the closet—the relations of the known and the unknown,
> the explicit and the inexplicit around homo/heterosexual

definition—have the potential for being peculiarly revealing, in fact, about speech acts more generally.

Sedgwick notes that homosexuality is considered inferior to
heterosexuality, but that the term "heterosexuality" wouldn't
even exist without the category of homosexuality. The concept
of heterosexuality depends on the existence (and lower status)
of homosexuality. This observation is meant to deconstruct the
power relationship between the two and deconstruct heteronormativity itself.

According to Sedgwick, viewing binaries like this is a way
to break down concepts of superiority and inferiority. It leads
her to highlight and exploit what she sees as the tension that
arises from holding two seemingly contradictory views at the
same time. In sexuality, for Sedgwick, these views are the "minoritizing view" and the "universalizing view."

In the *minoritizing view*, homosexuality is seen as the minority while heterosexuality is the majority. In the *universalizing view*, sexuality is considered a spectrum on which everybody has a place. That is, everybody is a little bit (or a lot) gay,
while also being a little bit (or a lot) straight. This seems contradictory, but Sedgwick believes that the contradiction itself is
useful. Endorsing two conflicting models of sexuality at once
can help us accept the complexity and mutability of sexuality.

We see here, yet again, the rejection of objective truth and
concrete categories and the idea that fluidity is liberating and
politically necessary. Queer Theorists can expand this thinking
to encompass almost anything, thereby "queering" the topic.

The Postmodern Principles and Themes in Queer Theory

Queer Theory is one of the most explicitly postmodern forms of Theory within identity studies today, owing many of its foundational concepts to Foucault. The postmodern knowledge principle, in which objective reality is denied or ignored, and the postmodern political principle, which insists that society is structured of systems of power and privilege that determine what is understood as knowledge, are front and center in queer Theory. They're most evident in the belief that science is an oppressive discipline that enforces gender conformity and heterosexuality by establishing categories and asserting their truth with rigorous authority and social pressure.

Of the four postmodern themes, the blurring of boundaries and the intense focus on language (discourses) are absolutely central to queer Theory. These are the two themes most hostile to the concept of a stable reality. The blurring of boundaries is queer Theory's preferred form of political activism ("queering"). The focus on language leads to an obsession with the ways sex, gender, and sexuality are spoken about, hence the recent explosion in the number of terms to describe subtle differences in gender identity and sexuality—like demisexual, asexual, and graysexual, which all describe very similar things. Queer Theory sees sexuality as an extremely fluid and changeable thing that demands impossibly extreme sensitivity of language. This leads, in turn, to a tendency to turn *what people do* into *who people are* within queer Theory. For example, many romantic styles or even fetishes or kinks are turned into *identi-*

ties, which are indicative of who people "really are" under this mode of thinking. This has the effect of making it impossible to question or criticize someone's behaviors—even those that might be harmful—without potentially offending them as a person or "denying them the right to exist."

The other two of the four themes also appear in queer Theory, but less overtly. The theme of cultural relativism is implicit—queer Theory assumes that understandings of gender and sexuality are always cultural constructs. It shares this with postcolonial Theory: queer Theorists often use postcolonial Theory and vice versa. There are significant differences between the two groups and their goals, but these two Theories often draw upon one another because their methods are both heavily influenced by Foucault and Derrida. The loss of the individual and the universal is also present: the individual's gendered and sexual self is considered to be constructed by discourses of power that they can't help but learn and can only subvert.

Because of its focus on deconstruction and its idea of knowledge as a construct of power, queer Theory may be the purest form of applied postmodernism. It forms the foundation of a lot of trans activism and makes an appearance in multiple forms of Critical Social Justice scholarship. Although the term "intersectionality" is more associated with critical race Theorist Kimberlé Crenshaw, Judith Butler has also spoken of "intersections" with other forms of marginalized identity. For her, "gender intersects with racial, class, ethnic, sexual, and regional modalities of discursively constituted identities." Butler's queer Theory is easily integrated into intersectional thought, and intersectional feminists are also likely to include queer Theory in their work.

But queer Theory is fundamentally different from the liberal feminism and LGBT activism that came before it. The success of universal liberal approaches to freeing sexual minorities and gender-nonconforming people contradict queer Theory's claim that theirs is the only way. The liberal activism and thought that predates Theory focused on changing prejudiced attitudes by appealing to our shared humanity, and to universal liberal principles. Trans activism could also benefit from this, if queer Theory weren't actively trying to subvert universal liberalism.

Instead, queer Theory aims to modify or unmake our concepts of sex, gender, and sexuality, which alienates most members of the society it wants to change. Queer activists who rely on queer Theory tend to act with surprising entitlement and aggression by ridiculing mainstream sexualities and genders and depicting them as backward. People generally don't appreciate being told that their sex, gender, and sexuality aren't real, or are wrong, or bad—you would think queer Theorists would appreciate this better than anyone.

Calling heterosexuality a social construct completely ignores the reality that humans are a sexually reproducing species, and calling homosexuality a social construct neglects all the evidence that it's also a biological reality. Despite any "liberation" we could achieve by treating all sexualities as social constructs, it threatens to undo the progress made by lesbian and gay activists in countering the belief that their romantic and sexual attractions are a mere "lifestyle choice." While homosexuality would be an acceptable lifestyle to choose, all the evidence—and the overwhelming testimony of gay men and lesbians—indicates that it's not a choice. If we give ground to those who say it is, we risk future oppression of LGBT people by social conservatives, who may demand that they just "choose" heterosexuality instead.

Being dismissive, ironic, antiscientific, and incomprehensible by design doesn't make for very productive activism. People who want their sex, gender, or sexuality to be accepted as normal don't want to be continually told that considering things normal is problematic. Although queer Theory claims to advocate for lesbian, gay, bisexual, and transgender people, the majority of LGBT people either are not especially familiar with it or do not support its overall agenda.

As it continues to assert itself as the only legitimate way to study or discuss topics of gender, sex, and sexuality, queer Theory harms the causes it most wants to support.

5 CRITICAL RACE THEORY AND INTERSECTIONALITY

Ending Racism by Seeing It Everywhere, Always

Critical race Theory is as American as apple pie or baseball. Its ideas have been used outside the United States, too, but even then, they're often flavored by America's unique racial history.

Critical race Theory says that race is a social construct created to maintain white privilege and white supremacy. This idea began long before postmodernism. In the early twentieth century, African American sociologist, historian, and author W. E. B. Du Bois argued that the idea of biological race was used to explain social and cultural differences in order to perpetuate the unjust treatment of racial minorities, especially African Americans.

This is true. There are some average differences across human populations, such as in skin color, hair texture, eye shape, and relative susceptibility to certain diseases, but these differences aren't big enough to divide people into groups called "races." Biologists don't. Biologists speak of populations, whose genetic markers show slightly different evolutionary heritages, but reducing this to "race" is both wrong and detrimental.

The racial categories we commonly hear about don't actually map onto precise genetic lineages. Our contemporary idea of "race" also doesn't stand up historically. "Race" wasn't considered significant in earlier periods. The Bible, for example, was written over two thousand years ago in the Mediterranean region, where black, brown, and white people lived. It's filled with moralistic tribalism but makes almost no mention of skin color. In late medieval England, references to "black" people often just meant dark-haired Europeans, people we would think of as "white."

Race and racism as we understand them today were probably socially constructed by Europeans to morally justify European colonialism and the Atlantic slave trade. European historians have tracked the rise of color-based prejudice over the early modern period, from roughly 1500 to 1800, and found that religious prejudice gave way to prejudice based on race over the course of the 1600s.

In order to justify the kidnapping, exploitation, and abuses within slavery and colonialism, their victims had to be thought of as inferior or subhuman. Other people at other times practiced slavery, colonialism, and even genocidal imperialism, and they also justified these atrocities by characterizing enslaved and conquered people as inferior according to characteristics like skin, hair, and eye color, things which we associate with race today. In Europe and its colonies, however, a few key differences led to unique discrimination and dehumanization.

Until the 1500s, Europeans didn't think of racial characteristics as inherited. Before then, they assumed things like skin color were determined by environment. "Race," as an inherited category, was constructed by emerging forms of scholarship in what we today call the social sciences and natural sciences, although they hadn't yet separated into the disciplines we now call "anthropology," "sociology," and "biology," and they hadn't yet formed rigorous, evidence-based research methods. Very preliminary results from science were misapplied, and extremely oversimplified (biological) categories emerged: being black ("blackness") and being white ("whiteness"), to which value judgments were soon attached.

Enter racism as we generally understand it today, which derived from this *biological racism* of earlier centuries and makes prejudicial judgments about people based upon their being classified into these crude racial categories regardless of who they are as individuals.

The earliest challengers of racism were former American slaves, including Sojourner Truth and Frederick Douglass, in the 1800s. Later, in the twentieth century, influential race critics like W. E. B. Du Bois and Winthrop Jordan wrote of the history of color-based racism in the United States.

The work of these scholars and reformers should have been enough to expose racism for the ugly and unfounded ideology that it is, but belief in the racial supremacy of whites survived. This was especially extreme and long-lived in the American

South, where slavery remained an essential part of the economy and society until President Abraham Lincoln's emancipation of the slaves in 1863. This act ultimately led to the formal abolishment of slavery with ratification of the Thirteenth Amendment of the U.S. Constitution in 1865.

Jim Crow laws (state and local laws that enforced racial segregation), racial redlining (legal discriminatory practices, especially ones that prevented black people from living in certain neighborhoods), and legal segregation survived the longest, persisting into the mid-1960s and, in some ways, beyond. Even after the victories of the Civil Rights Movement under Dr. Martin Luther King, Jr., when racial discrimination became illegal and attitudes about race changed remarkably fast in historical terms, these longstanding narratives didn't disappear.

Critical race Theory was, according to its Theorists, designed to pick out, highlight, and address these narratives. It does this in a very particular way, though, which isn't the only way to challenge lingering racism.

Taking a Critical Approach

Critical race Theory formally arose in the 1970s, through the critical study of law as it relates to issues of race. The word *critical* here means that it's specifically geared toward identifying and exposing problems in order to bring about revolutionary political change. Despite legal changes that addressed racial discrimination, many activists felt a need to continue working on the racism that remained, which was less obvious. To accomplish this, they adopted Critical Theory approaches and, eventually, postmodern Theory.

The critical race approach has always been divided into at least two parts—the "materialist" and the "intersectional," which is more postmodern and seeks a synthesis between materialism and idealism. Materialist race critics theorize about how material systems—economic, legal, political—affect racial minorities. Idealists focus on how ideas and conceptions go on to shape society and the people who live within it. Intersectional Theorists are more concerned with linguistic and social systems and therefore aim to deconstruct discourses, detect implicit biases, and counter underlying racial assumptions and attitudes. They deem that these systems and structures have both material and psychological impacts significant enough to determine life outcomes in spite of individual traits like competence, values, and character.

Because of these differences in approach, some materialists have criticized idealists and intersectionalists for their obscure discourse analyses, which usually take place in elite academic settings and neglect widespread material issues like poverty. Idealists and intersectionalists counter that, while material reality is of practical importance, it can't be improved if discourses continue to oppress. All three approaches—materialist, idealist, and intersectional (postmodern) critical race Theorists— react against liberalism.

The late Derrick Bell, the first tenured African American professor at Harvard Law School, is often seen as the founder of critical race Theory, though he didn't name it. The Theory's name came later (in 1989, in fact) by inserting "race" into his area of specialty—critical legal studies—and into a broader Critical Theory critique of society. Though critical legal studies draws upon Marxism, Critical Theory, and even postmodernists like Jacques Derrida, Bell was largely a materialist, perhaps best known for applying critical methods to civil rights and the discourses surrounding them. Bell was an open advocate of historical revisionism and is best known for his "interest convergence" thesis, described in his 1970 book, *Race, Racism, and American Law.*

Interest convergence says that whites have only given rights to blacks when it was in their interest to do so—a dismal view that denies the moral progress made since the Jim Crow era. Bell states this explicitly in his 1987 book, *And We Are Not Saved: The Elusive Quest for Racial Justice*: "progress in American race relations is largely a mirage obscuring the fact that whites continue, consciously or unconsciously, to do all in their power to ensure their dominion and maintain their control."

Bell's work is full of this pessimism. Because he believed in a pervasive and irreparable system of white dominance in U.S. society (the subtitle of his 1992 book, *Faces at the Bottom of the Well*, is "The Permanence of Racism"), he argued that the new changes in civil rights led to a whole new set of circumstances in which white supremacy would continue to oppress black people. One example of this would be so-called white flight, a term that describes white people moving out of urban neighborhoods with high minority populations and into the (very white) suburbs. For Bell, racist conditions don't improve; they hide themselves better. Critical race Theory is the tool that was developed to find this "hidden" racism that Bell's pessimism assumed must exist in virtually every situation.

Of course, the materialists were right about some things: legal equality between races isn't enough to resolve all inequalities. There's still work to be done not only in the legal sphere but also in the political and economic spheres to address imbalances: unequal school funding in majority black areas, harsher sentencing of black offenders, disparities in housing and lending to black people, and differences in representations of black people in high-prestige jobs. This all must be done with a view to learning how these disparities happen. In this regard, Bell's work (especially his earlier work) is often insightful, despite its pessimistic and cynical disposition.

On the other hand, there's plenty to criticize about the materialists. They frequently advocate Black Nationalism and segregation over universal human rights and cooperation. Their supposedly evidence-based analyses of material reality, which usually find that racism and discrimination are not decreasing at all, can look a great deal like cherry-picking and generalizing from the worst examples. Their strong advocacy for expanding positive discrimination programs, like affirmative action, are often seen by critics as divisive, counterproductive, and a form of soft bigotry that holds racial minorities in low esteem and unable to compete on their individual merits.

Materialists dominated the critical race movement from the 1970s to the 1980s, but from the 1990s, intersectionalists became increasingly dominant, incorporating significant amounts of postmodernism into what was by then recognized as critical race Theory. Over time, the postmodernists came to focus on microaggressions, hate speech, safe spaces, cultural appropriation, implicit association tests, media representation, "whiteness," and all the now familiar terms of racial discourse.

A number of female critical Theorists who gained prominence in the late 1980s and 1990s—and who promoted radical black feminist thought—were responsible for this change. These scholars include bell hooks (whose name is intentionally spelled in all lowercase letters), Audre Lorde, and Patricia Hill Collins. They blurred the boundaries of different disciplines, arguing passionately about both patriarchy and white supremacy in ways that mixed legal analysis with sociological, literary, and autobiographical approaches.

Significantly, they complained about the "whiteness" of feminism, setting the stage for another wave of influential Theorists: Patricia Williams, Angela Harris, and Kimberlé Crenshaw—a student of Derrick Bell who created the term "critical race Theory" at the first official meeting of critical race Theorists in Madison, Wisconsin, in 1989. These scholars drew on critical race Theory and feminism, which included ideas about gender and sexuality. This produced a layered, sophisticated analysis of identity and experience, which included social, legal, and economic factors. By looking at multiple systems of power and privilege and seeing experience as a source of knowledge about those systems, they moved away from studying the material realities of racism, especially poverty, and instead focused on discourses and power.

Critical race Theory also started to lean heavily into identity politics and standpoint theory—the idea that your identity and position in society, particularly if you're a minority, can make your point of view more legitimate than the points of view of others. This idea is central to critical race Theory. It shows up in the very first lines of *The Alchemy of Race and Rights,* the 1991 book-length essay by Patricia Williams, a professor of commercial law: "[S]ubject position is everything in my analysis of the law." That is, your race and other identity-based factors are to be considered *everything* to your standing under the law, even in a society with legal equality in which several Civil Rights Acts had already been passed by the U.S. Congress, including, perhaps most notably, the Civil Rights Act of 1964, a landmark piece of legislation that explicitly prohibits discrimination on the basis of race, color, religion, sex, or national origin.

Unusually for Theory, critical race Theory's writings are quite clear. The frustrating postmodern language of postcolonial and queer Theories is mostly absent—this is probably because critical race Theory came out of legal studies. It still believes in the importance of discourse in constructing social reality, but it doesn't often tie itself up in endless word games. It's easy to figure out the tenets of critical race Theory—in fact, its scholars enjoy listing them. For example, the highly influential reader *Critical Race Theory: An Introduction*, by Richard Delgado and Jean Stefancic, first published in 2001, sets out the core tenets:

- "Racism is ordinary, not aberrational." That is, it is the everyday experience of people of color in the United States.

- "[A] system of white-over-color ascendancy serves important purposes, both psychic and material, for the dominant group." That is, white supremacy is systemic and benefits white people. Therefore, "color-blind" policies can tackle only the most egregious and demonstrable forms of discrimination.

- "[T]he 'social construction' thesis holds that race and races are products of social thought and relations." Intersectionality and antiessentialism—opposition to the idea of racial difference as innate—are needed to address this.

- A "unique voice of color" exists and "minority status . . . brings with it a presumed competence to speak about race and racism." This is not understood as essentialism but as the product of common experiences of oppression. In other words, this is standpoint theory.

These core tenets plainly describe what's going on in critical race Theory—racism is present everywhere and always, and persistently works against people of color, who are aware of this, and for the benefit of white people, who tend not to be, because of their privilege. Other Theorists and educators include a fundamental distrust of liberalism, a rejection of meritocracy, and a commitment to Critical Social Justice.

The Spread of Critical Race Theory

Critical race Theory has expanded out of legal studies and into many disciplines concerned with social justice–related issues. Pedagogy (the theory of education) has been particularly strongly affected. As Delgado and Stefancic observe in *Critical Race Theory: An Introduction,*

> Although CRT [critical race Theory] began as a movement in the law, it has rapidly spread beyond that discipline. Today, many scholars in the field of education consider themselves critical race theorists who use CRT's ideas to understand issues of school discipline and hierarchy, tracking, affirmative action, high-stakes testing, controversies over curriculum and history, bilingual and multicultural education, and alternative and charter schools.

They list critical race Theory's strongest footholds: political science, women's studies, ethnic studies, American studies, sociology, theology, health care, and philosophy. They further note how critical race Theory takes an unapologetically activist stance:

> Unlike some academic disciplines, critical race theory contains an activist dimension. It tries not only to understand our social situation but to change it, setting out not only to ascertain how society organizes itself along racial lines and hierarchies but to transform it for the better.

As a result, activists in all walks of life speak the language of critical race Theory. But when you listen to that language, you might come away thinking that critical race Theory itself sounds a bit racist. Here are some common lines of thought in critical race Theory:

- White people are inherently racist.

- Racism is "prejudice plus power," so only white people can be racist because they have all the institutional power.

- Only people of color can talk about racism—white people need to just listen.

- Being "colorblind" is, in fact, racist, because it ignores the pervasive racism that dominates society and perpetuates white privilege.

- Racism is embedded in culture and we can't escape it.

While you have likely encountered these mantras online or in the media—including those mantras that ascribe profound failures of morals and character to white people—they are particularly prevalent on college campuses. Indeed, Critical race Theory has become a significant part of campus culture in many universities, especially at the most elite institutions. Intersectionality is central to this culture and has also taken on a life of its own outside it.

Despite critical race Theory's focus on discourses, attitudes, and bias, some scholars have doubted whether critical race Theory is postmodern. One common objection is that postmodernism typically rejects shared meaning and stable identity (or "subjecthood"). Identity politics doesn't make much sense from a strict postmodern perspective.

Critics making this argument have a point, but in the late 1980s and early 1990s, critical race Theorists did take some core ideas from postmodernism's deconstructive phase (which Kimberlé Crenshaw called the "vulgar constructionist" approach in her highly influential paper "Mapping the Margins") and adapted them into a new, politically applicable project, even as these same Theorists rejected endless deconstruction as a symptom of the privilege of white male philosophers like Foucault and Derrida. Black feminist scholar and activist bell hooks, for example, wrote in the 1980s that those original postmodernists who wanted to get rid of coherent voices and subjecthood, or a sense of shared meaning and stable identity, were wealthy white men, a group of privilege whose voices had already been heard and whose identity was dominant in society.

In Angela Harris's influential 1990 essay, "Race and Essentialism in Feminist Legal Theory," she likewise argues that feminism failed black women by treating their experience as just a variation on white women's experience. These ideas developed into a core line of thought in critical race Theory called *intersectionality*.

Intersectionality

Intersectionality began as a heuristic—a tool that lets someone discover something for themselves. Its creator, Kimberlé Crenshaw, now describes it as a "practice."

She first introduced intersectionality in a controversial 1989 scholarly law paper called "Demarginalizing the Intersection of Race and Sex: A Black Feminist Critique of Antidiscrimination Doctrine, Feminist Theory and Antiracist Politics." In it, she examines three legal discrimination cases and uses the metaphor of a roadway intersection to examine the ways in which different forms of prejudice can "hit" an individual with two or more marginalized identities.

She argues that—just as someone standing in the intersection of two streets could get hit by a car coming from any direction or even by more than one at a time—a marginalized person may not be able to tell which of their identities is being discriminated against in any given instance. Crenshaw argues persuasively that laws to prevent discrimination on the grounds of race *or* gender aren't enough to deal with this problem or with the fact that a black woman, for instance, might experience unique forms of discrimination that neither white women nor black men face.

This idea was about to change the world. Two years later, Crenshaw fleshed it out further in her highly influential 1991 essay, "Mapping the Margins: Intersectionality, Identity Politics, and Violence against Women of Color," in which she defines intersectionality as a "provisional concept linking contemporary politics with postmodern theory." For Crenshaw, a postmodern approach to intersectionality allowed critical race Theory and feminism to incorporate political activism while still considering race and gender cultural constructs.

This approach allowed for more and more categories of marginalized identity to be considered in intersectional analysis—sexuality, gender identity, disability status, etc.—adding more and more layers to the concept and the scholarship and activism that use it. This complexity spurred two decades of fresh activity by scholars and activists. "Mapping the Margins" paved the way by openly advocating identity politics over liberal universalism, which focuses on treating people equally regardless of identity.

Identity politics emphasizes the importance of identity categories as sources of empowerment and community. Rejecting the idea of shared universal humanity explicitly, Crenshaw writes:

> We all can recognize the distinction between the claims "I am Black" and the claim "I am a person who happens to be Black." "I am Black" takes the socially imposed identity and empowers it as an anchor of subjectivity. "I am Black" becomes not simply a statement of resistance but also a positive discourse of self-identification, intimately linked to celebratory statements like the Black nationalist "Black is beautiful." "I am a person who happens to be Black," on the other hand, achieves self-identification by straining for a certain universality (in effect, "I am first a person") and for a concomitant dismissal of the imposed category ("Black") as contingent, circumstantial, nondeterminant.

Because of that focus on the social significance of race and gender, "Mapping the Margins" is central to Critical Social Justice today. It draws on postmodern cultural constructivism, while still considering oppression objectively real and advocating actionable political goals. It's the clearest, most classic example of how applied postmodernism emerged and evolved in the late 1980s and early 1990s. The central feature of that evolution is that it adopts the view that it is inappropriate, if not impossible, to deconstruct identity categories that are considered within Theory to be sites of systemic oppression.

Intersectionality and the Applied Postmodern Turn

In "Mapping the Margins," Crenshaw critiques both the universal liberal and high-deconstructive postmodernist viewpoints.

Liberalism seeks to remove social expectations from identity categories—black people being expected to do menial jobs, women being expected to prioritize domestic and parenting roles over careers, and so on—and make all rights, freedoms, and opportunities available to all people *regardless* of their identity. There's a strong focus on the individual, and identity categories are less important. To Crenshaw, this is unacceptable. She writes,

> [For] African Americans, other people of color, and gays and lesbians, among others ... identity-based politics has been a source of strength, community, and intellectual development. The embrace of identity politics, however, has been in tension with dominant conceptions of social justice. Race, gender, and other identity categories are most often treated in mainstream liberal discourse as vestiges of bias or domination—that is, as intrinsically negative frameworks in which social power works to exclude or marginalize those who are different. According to this understanding, our liberatory objective should be to empty such categories of any social significance. Yet implicit in certain strands of feminist and racial liberation movements, for example, is the view

that the social power in delineating difference need not be
the power of domination; it can instead be the source of social empowerment and reconstruction.

Crenshaw is talking about a major change here. At the
height of its deconstructive phase, postmodernism helped us
analyze power structures and, in Crenshaw's view, usefully understand race and gender as social constructs. But its skepticism was too extreme to allow the reality of social structures
and categories, which have to be acknowledged if we want to
address discrimination. She thus criticizes that aspect of radically deconstructive postmodernism, while insisting that the
postmodern political principle is otherwise convincing:

> While the descriptive project of postmodernism of ques-
> tioning the ways in which meaning is socially constructed
> is generally sound, this critique sometimes misreads the
> meaning of social construction and distorts its political rel-
> evance. . . . But to say that a category such as race or gender
> is socially constructed is not to say that that category has no
> significance in our world. On the contrary, a large and con-
> tinuing project for subordinated people—and indeed, one
> of the projects for which postmodern theories have been
> very helpful—is thinking about the way power has clustered
> around certain categories and is exercised against others.

Crenshaw proposed a way of thinking that accepted that
complex layers of discrimination objectively exist and so do
categories of people and systems of power—even if they have
been socially constructed. These, she writes in "Mapping the

Margins," are *imposed* by those with power onto oppressed groups and cannot merely be deconstructed.

This is intersectionality. It explicitly embraces the postmodern political principle—the belief that society consists of systems of power—and a variant of the postmodern knowledge principle, which sees knowledge as being related to your position in society. Crenshaw's intersectionality rejected individualism in favor of group identity, and intersectional feminists and critical race Theorists have continued to do the same ever since.

Complex, Yet So Very Simple

Since the invention of intersectionality, its meaning and purpose have expanded hugely. The number of identity groups you can use to divide people can be almost infinite—but under intersectionality, no matter how very specific their identities are, they never just become unique individuals. Even if a person is a unique mix of marginalized identities, they're understood through each and all of those identities, not as an individual.

In addition to the categories of race, sex, class, sexuality, gender identity, religion, immigration status, physical ability, mental health, and body size, there are subcategories such as exact skin tone, exact body shape, and exact gender identity and sexuality, which number in the hundreds. These all have to be understood in relation to one another so that each intersection can be analyzed. This isn't just complicated—it's also completely subjective, because not all identity categories have the same levels of marginalization or are even comparable.

There's nothing complex about the overarching idea of intersectionality, or the Theories it's built on. It does the same thing over and over again: it looks for the power imbalances, bigotry, and biases that it assumes are present and picks at them. It reduces *everything* to prejudice. Different outcomes between groups can have one, and only one, explanation, and that's prejudicial bigotry.

The only question is how to identify it.

The Caste System of Critical Social Justice

Intersectionality is full of divisions and subcategories, which often conflict with each other. Here are some examples:

- Gay white men and non-black people of color are told they need to recognize their privilege over gay men of color and black people.

- Lighter-skinned black people are told to recognize their privilege over darker-skinned black people.

- Straight black men have been described as the "white people of black people."

It's also becoming more common to hear people argue that trans men, though still oppressed by attitudes toward trans people, now have male privilege and need to amplify the voices of trans women, who are seen as doubly oppressed because they're both trans and women. Gay men and lesbians might soon find themselves not considered oppressed at all, particularly if they are not attracted to trans men or trans women, which is considered transphobic. Asians and Jews are losing their "marginalized" status due to their economic success, which is attributed to their participation in "whiteness" or other factors like self-interest and a rejection of intersectional solidarity. Queerness needs to be decolonized and its conceptual origins in white figures like Judith Butler need to be "interrogated."

In the real world, it's not always possible to respect all marginalized identities at once. When lifelong human rights campaigner Peter Tatchell criticized black rappers who sang about murdering gay people, he was accused of racism. A similar thing happened in British Columbia, Canada, when ethnic minority beauticians declined bikini wax services to a trans woman on the grounds that their religion and customs prohibited contact with male genitals. In that situation, you can't support minority women's rights and trans women's rights at the same time.

Because of how versatile intersectionality is, it's an appealing tool for those involved in many different forms of engagement, ranging from legal activism and academic analysis to affirmative action and educational theory. Mainstream activism has also eagerly embraced intersectionality—especially the concept of *privilege*, an idea that's often used as a weapon against those perceived as powerful.

The Meme of Critical Social Justice

In her book *Intersectionality: An Intellectual History*, Ange-Marie Hancock describes intersectionality's growing popularity in both the intellectual and academic realms. In popular culture, Hancock notes, intersectionality is often evoked to *cancel* people, and public figures from Michelle Obama to members of the feminist group Code Pink have been criticized for failing "to understand and act from a place deeply cognizant of the multicategory dynamics of power at play."

Intersectionality has truly gone viral. It's taken on new and unexpected applications, especially in activism. In 2017, Kimberlé Crenshaw observed that intersectionality had expanded beyond what she had originally intended. Instead of doing anything to alleviate actual oppression, though, it has become more of a way to describe how complicated issues of identity can be. She hasn't stopped advocating for it, though.

In addition to its confusing, highly interpretive Theoretical approach, intersectionality, along with critical race Theory more broadly, is characterized by a great deal of divisiveness, pessimism, and cynicism. Its paranoid mind-set—which assumes racism is everywhere, always, just waiting to be found—is unlikely to be helpful or healthy for those who adopt it. Always believing that you will be or are being discriminated against, and trying to find out how, is unlikely to improve the outcome of any situation.

It can also be self-defeating. In *The Coddling of the American Mind*, attorney Greg Lukianoff and social psychologist Jonathan Haidt describe this mind-set as a kind of reverse cognitive behavioral therapy (CBT), a type of mental health treatment shown to be effective. The main purpose of CBT is to train yourself *not* to interpret every situation in the most negative light. The goal is to develop a more positive and re-silient attitude toward the world, so that you can engage with it as fully as possible. If young people are trained to see insult, hostility, and prejudice in every interaction, they'll begin to see the world as hostile to them and won't thrive in it.

Noble Ends, Terrible Means

Critical race Theory is centrally concerned with ending rac-ism, through the unlikely means of making everyone aware of race at all times and places. Its core assumption is that—no matter what people actually think, believe, say, or do—racism is normal and permanent. As scholar-activists Heather Bruce, Robin DiAngelo, Gyda Swaney, and Amie Thurber put it at the influential Race and Pedagogy National Conference at the University of Puget Sound in 2014, "The question is not 'did racism take place?'"—because, for them, that's seen as obvi-ous—"but rather 'how did racism manifest in that situation?'" That is, we should all examine each and every situation for evidence of the racism that is always present.

Here are just some of the core problems with critical race Theory:

- It places social importance on race, which inflames racism instead of stopping it.

- It tends to be purely Theoretical and not very practical, especially with its uses of the postmodern knowledge and political principles.

- It's aggressive.

- It asserts that racism is pervasive and omnipresent, dwelling just beneath the surface in all interactions and social phenomena.

Seeing racism as omnipresent and eternal grants it a mythological status, like sin or depravity. Members of marginalized racial groups are said to have a unique voice and a counternarrative that, under Theory, *must* be regarded as authoritative because it is "authentic" (this is the postmodern knowledge principle). Because of this, their reading of any situation can't be disputed (unless they happen to be one of the very many members of "marginalized" racial groups who don't agree with critical race Theory). Everything the Theoretically orthodox marginalized individual interprets as racism is considered racism by default.

In scholarship, this leads to theories built only upon theories with no real way of testing or falsifying them. Adherents actively search for hidden and overt racial offenses until they find them, and they allow no alternative explanations. Racism is inevitable but also unforgivable. This can lead to mob outrage and public shaming ("cancel culture").

Interpreting everything as racist is unlikely to produce the desired results. Some studies have already shown that diversity courses, in which members of dominant groups are told that racism is everywhere and that they themselves enable it, have resulted in increased hostility toward marginalized groups. It's bad psychology to tell people who don't believe they're racist—

who likely even actively despise racism—that there is nothing they can do to stop themselves from being racist. It's even less helpful to set up double-bind or no-win situations, in which people are given two conflicting messages that present an unresolvable dilemma—for example, telling someone that it is racist to notice race, because only someone who is racist notices race, but that it is also racist not to notice race, because only someone with privilege has the luxury of not noticing race.

By focusing so intently on race and objecting to "color-blindness"—the refusal to attach social significance to race—critical race Theory threatens to undo the social taboo we have built up against judging people by their race. An obsessive focus on race is not likely to end well—neither for minority groups nor for social cohesion.

6 FEMINISMS AND GENDER STUDIES
Performing and Problematizing

Feminism has been one of the most successful social movements in human history. Over the past century alone, the strides made in liberating just over half the population have been amazing.

But something changed in feminism around the year 2000: a surprising number of activists took up a new approach—intersectionality, which combined many forms of identity Theory. The liberal, materialist, and radical approaches to feminism, which had dominated for much of the previous century, were almost totally displaced by the new intersectional approach.

From the outside, the intersectional approach seems grating, fractious, and needlessly complicated. It appears to continually undermine itself over petty differences and grievances. It does this through calls for the various oppressed tribes to support each other under the banner of "allyship"—which is then Theorized as problematic because it "centers" the needs of more privileged allies at the expense of oppressed minority groups. It seems impossible for even those who believe in intersectionality to do anything right.

Feminisms Then and Now

Feminism, in its most basic definition, means "belief in equality between the sexes." By that definition, the majority of the population is now feminist. Feminist scholarship and activism, however, have always been much more ideological and theoretical, and the dominant ideologies and theories have changed dramatically over time—accompanied by a lot of infighting.

Feminism, in the political and philosophical sense, includes a dizzying number of branches: radical cultural feminists, radical lesbian feminists, radical libertarian feminists, separatists, French psychoanalytical feminists, womanists, liberal feminists, neoliberal feminists, socialist/materialist feminists, Marxist feminists, Islamic feminists, Christian feminists, Jewish feminists, choice feminists, equity feminists, postfeminists, black feminists, and intersectional feminists. All these groups are interested in women's rights, roles, and experiences in society, but they differ widely on how they understand these.

We'll be discussing four broad areas of feminist thought: liberal feminism, radical feminism, materialist (effectively socialist) feminism, and intersectional feminism.

Liberal feminism was the most broad-based activist form during feminism's "second wave," from the late 1960s through the mid-1980s. Radical and materialist feminisms differ from liberal feminism but overlap with each other. They're some-what competing scholarly branches of feminism, dominant during the same period, with radical feminists placing more emphasis on patriarchy and materialist feminists placing more on capitalism, but both placing significant emphasis on both. Intersectional feminism is the new variant, which replaced the others in scholarly and activist arenas from the mid-1990s on-ward.

Liberal feminism worked incrementally to extend all the rights and freedoms of a liberal society to women. It success-fully reshaped the landscape of society, particularly in the workplace. The other two feminisms were also present in ac-tivism and more dominant in feminist scholarship. Materialist feminists were concerned with class and how patriarchy and capitalism act together to constrain women, especially in the workplace and the home. Their theories drew on Marxism and socialism. Radical feminists focused on patriarchy and viewed men and women as classes, with women as the oppressed and men as the oppressors. They were revolutionaries who aimed to remake society, dismantle the concept of gender (but *not* sex), and overthrow both patriarchy and capitalism.

These three main branches developed differently in differ-ent places. It's important to understand that the liberal femi-nist approach got the most support from society, but radical and materialist feminism dominated in universities, especially from the 1970s onward.

This began to change in the late 1980s and 1990s, when a new crop of Theorists successfully packaged a more "sophis-

ticated" approach—postmodern Theory—for a new generation of activists. This approach was applied postmodernism,
which accepted identity oppression as "real" and thus brought
postmodernism into feminist activism. It incorporated aspects
of queer Theory, postcolonial Theory, and critical race Theory
through the concept of intersectionality.

These new developments changed the character of feminism both in the popular consciousness and in the academy.
This "third-wave" of feminism tended to neglect class issues
and focus on identity in the form of race, gender, and sexuality. Instead of rallying around the shared identity of women as
a "sisterhood," intersectional and queer feminisms deny that
women have common experiences and complicate what it even
means to be a woman. While liberal feminists wanted the freedom to reject gender roles and access the same opportunities
as men, and radical feminists had wanted to dismantle gender
entirely as an oppressive social construct, intersectional feminists saw gender as both culturally constructed and as something that people could experience as real and expect to have
acknowledged as such.

An "Increasingly Sophisticated" Theory

By the early 2000s, the intersectional shift in feminism had become undeniable. In a 2006 essay, Judith Lorber, a professor
(now emerita) of sociology and gender studies, summarized
the four main tendencies of this shift in an essay titled "Shifting
Paradigms and Challenging Categories":

1. Making gender—not biological sex—central.

2. Treating gender and sexuality as social constructs.

3. Reading power into those constructions—power that acts in the Foucauldian sense of a permeating grid.

4. Focusing on *standpoint*—that is, identity.

Lorber called these changes an "increasingly sophisticated" model for feminist thought. They are, in truth, the direct result of applied postmodern Theory. Each of the four points embodies the postmodern knowledge principle and the postmodern political principle. In this new feminist view, knowledge is "situated," which means that it comes from one's "standpoint" in society, by which Theorists mean one's membership in intersecting identity groups. This ties knowledge to power and both knowledge and power to the discourses that create, maintain, and legitimize dominance and oppression within society.

Like in critical race Theory, intersectionality offered activists a renewed sense of purpose, as it provided them with new problems to interrogate and new accusations to make— especially against each other. For example, the black feminist thought and critical race Theory that informed this shift accused feminism of being "white" and of ignoring problems relevant to race, due to the corrupting influences of white privilege.

Meanwhile, queer feminist thought accused feminism of being exclusionary of first lesbian, then LGB, then LGBT, and later LGBTQ issues, because of heteronormativity and the associated privileges. This led care-oriented scholars to become increasingly "woke" not only to the ways in which others are oppressed but also to the ways feminism itself could be Theorized to have contributed to or been complicit in oppression.

Ultimately, this last concern was subsumed into *gender studies*, which draws upon and informs feminist thinking, but is technically distinct from it.

The development of gender studies has its own story. The academic study of gender emerged in the 1950s and 1960s, mainly from literary theory. At first, it was simply called "women's studies," because it looked at women's issues and advocated the political empowerment of women.

Some key texts included Simone de Beauvoir's *The Second Sex* (1949), a groundbreaking book that argued that women are constructed by the cultural understanding that they're inferior to men, and Betty Friedan's *The Feminine Mystique* (1963), which criticized the idea that women were fulfilled by domesticity and motherhood. Kate Millet's *Sexual Politics* (1970) provided a close reading of negative representations of women in literary texts by men, and Germaine Greer's *The Female Eunuch* (1970) argued that women were sexually repressed and alienated from their own bodies and unaware of how much men hated them. These texts all fall within radical feminism, arguing that womanhood is culturally constructed and imposed by men (in a top-down power dynamic), and advocate the revolutionary overthrow of patriarchy.

In the 1970s and much of the 1980s, feminist scholars looked closely at women's roles in the family and workforce and at social expectations that women be feminine, submis-

sive, and beautiful—either that, or sexually available and por-
nographic. Marxist ideas of women as a subordinated class that
exists to produce male workers (who, in turn, support capitalism) inspired many feminists who met for "consciousness-
raising" sessions to fully understand their culturally constructed oppression. This followed from the (neo-)Marxist concept
of "false consciousness," which means ways of thinking that
prevent someone from being able to know the realities of her
situation. This is similar to the newer concept of "internalized
misogyny," which describes women who accept the social enforcement of women's inferiority as normal and natural.

However, in the late 1980s and early 1990s, the landscape
began to change, as the applied postmodern influence of queer
Theory, postcolonial Theory, and intersectionality began to
make itself felt.

As Lorber describes in her 2006 essay, Marxist feminism
saw women as a *class*. She argues that, after addressing inequalities in the workplace through the 1970s and early 1980s,
"Marxist feminists expanded their analysis to show that the
exploitation of housewives was an integral part of the capitalist economy." This materialist feminist view presents a metanarrative about men, women, and society, based on a simple
oppressive male/oppressed female binary.

Such a binary was unacceptable to the postmodern Theorists. The new Theorists, who gained influence over feminist
thought in the late 1980s, drew on queer Theory to challenge
the categories of "women" and "men" at their very foundations.
By the early 2000s, the dominant view was that—because gen-

der has been constructed differently by dominant discourses at different times and places—it doesn't make sense to use the words "women" and "men" at all. They argued that, under Theory, "'women' and 'men' are regarded as constructions or representations—achieved through discourse, performance, and repetition—rather than 'real' entities."

In other words, feminism gave way to gender studies in order to include more and more oppressed identities and adopted intersectionality as a kind of grand unifying Theory. Gender studies viewed knowledge as a cultural construct (the postmodern knowledge principle), worked within many vectors of power and privilege (the postmodern political principle), and was deconstructing categories, blurring boundaries, focusing on discourses, practicing cultural relativism, and honoring identity-group wisdom (the four postmodern themes).

Why might have such a change occurred within feminism? For more hints, let's focus a bit more on the four aspects of the paradigm shift that Lorber identified in her 2006 essay:

1. *Making gender—not biological sex—central.* Feminists no longer saw the world as "women" versus "men." Therefore, "patriarchy" no longer made sense as the enemy. Instead, using Foucauldian ideas, the problem was that male dominance permeated discourse. The new paradigm saw power and privilege as an "organizing principle."

2. *Treating gender and sexuality as social constructs.* Gender became something we do to ourselves and each other. Like "to queer," which emerged as a verb in queer Theory, "to

gender" became a verb. For example, before the applied postmodern turn, an advertisement showing a woman using dishwashing detergent might have been seen as reinforcing patriarchal expectations and exploiting women in a material sense. After the shift, it came to be seen as a way of "gendering" domestic tasks, using discourses to legitimize the idea that washing dishes is part of what it means to be a woman.

3. *Reading power into those constructions.* Ideas about the ways in which feminine roles are subordinate to masculine ones remained, but understanding these roles moved from a focus on legal, economic, and political factors and on the overtly sexist expectations of women by men to a focus on more subtle, interactional, learned, performed, and internalized expectations perpetuated by everybody. This is the postmodern view of power promoted by Michel Foucault.

4. *Focusing on* standpoint—*that is, identity.* Standpoint theory and intersectionality became central to feminist knowledge production. "Women's studies"—which was based on biological sex categories and the construction of gender in the service of capitalism—had largely become "gender studies," which is strongly postmodern.

Intersectional Theory provided this new and "increasingly sophisticated" way to understand power dynamics in society for a simple yet important reason: the previous incarnations of feminism were so successful there wasn't much work left for feminism to do. Patriarchal men with sexist beliefs still existed, but it became increasingly difficult to view Western society as genuinely patriarchal or to see most men as actively misogynistic. Postmodern Theory offered an opportunity to keep the same beliefs and predictions—male domination exists and serves itself at the expense of women—while redefining them so the work to change society could continue.

We often see this kind of shift to a more "sophisticated" and nebulous technique when people are very personally and ideologically attached to a theory that is clearly failing. This phenomenon was first described by American social psychologist Leon Festinger in his study of UFO cults, and led to the development of the concept of *cognitive dissonance*. Festinger observed that committed members of cults didn't abandon their beliefs when the cult's predictions failed to come true. Instead, cultists would claim the event *had* occurred, but in some unfalsifiable way (specifically, they claimed God decided to spare the planet as a result of the faith of the cultists).

Doing Gender Studies

So what's being studied in gender studies? Pretty much everything. Gender studies overlaps with so many different scholarly disciplines that its scholars study practically everything that humans typically engage in. They apply intersectionality, queer Theory, and postcolonial Theory and thus, ultimately, postmodern conceptions of knowledge, power, and discourses.

Take "gendering," for example. "Gendering" is seen as an oppressive action, but not as something powerful individuals do knowingly. Instead, it's created by social interactions on all levels, interactions that become more and more complex as further layers of identity are added to the mix. In their massively influential 1987 paper, "Doing Gender"—the most cited work in gender studies, which has contributed to over thirteen thousand other academic papers, articles, and books since its first publication—Candace West and Don H. Zimmerman aimed "to advance a new understanding of gender as a routine accomplishment embedded in everyday interaction." They write,

> We contend that the "doing" of gender is undertaken by women and men whose competence as members of society is hostage to its production. Doing gender involves a complex of socially guided perceptual, interactional, and micropolitical activities that cast particular pursuits as expressions of masculine and feminine "natures."

West and Zimmerman explicitly reject biology as a source of differences in male and female behaviors, preferences, or traits, noting,

> Doing gender means creating differences between girls and boys and women and men, differences that are not natural, essential, or biological. Once the differences have been constructed, they are used to reinforce the "essentialness" of gender.

In Judith Butler's iconic work *Gender Trouble*, which emerged at around the same time as "Doing Gender" and drew on Foucault's ideas about the construction of sexuality, gender is learned and reproduced, like language. West and Zimmerman understand gender in roughly the same way.

In 1995, the concept of gender as something that is "done" was given a more intersectional slant by Candace West and Sarah Fenstermaker. In a follow-up essay to "Doing Gender," called "Doing Difference," West and Fenstermaker look at the intersections of gender with race and class. Since then, gender studies has attempted to take an increasing number of diverse identities into account, particularly as trans studies has become more relevant.

The Death of Liberal Feminism

Liberal feminism works alongside secular, liberal democracy, individual agency within a framework of universal human rights, and an Enlightenment focus on reason and science. This made it the explicit, central target of postmodernists. Liberal feminists generally believe society already provides almost all the opportunities required for women to succeed in life. They just need the same access to those opportunities as men, along with measures that allow and protect that access—educational opportunities, affordable childcare, flexible working hours, and so on. Liberal feminists want to preserve the structures and institutions of secular, liberal democracy and open them up.

The intersectional feminists want a shift toward "mutual respect" and "affirmation of difference," that is, a sense of solidarity and allyship among marginalized groups. This means respect for differences between social and cultural groups, not for individuals with different viewpoints. This requires cultural relativism and standpoint theory—the view that belonging to a marginalized group provides special access to truth, by allowing members insight into both dominance and their own oppression.

The understanding that different groups have different experiences, beliefs, and values was largely influenced by black feminists who criticized second-wave feminism for not recognizing that black women faced different prejudices and stereotypes than white women. bell hooks' 1982 book, *Ain't I a Woman?*, was very influential in this regard. On the topic of black women's place in the feminist movement, hooks says,

> When the women's movement began in the late 60s, it was evident that the white women who dominated the movement felt it was "their" movement, that is the medium through which a white woman would voice her grievance to society. Not only did white women act as if feminist ideology existed solely to serve their own interests because they were able to draw public attention to feminist concerns. They were unwilling to acknowledge that non-white women were part of the collective group women in American society.

In her 1990 book, *Black Feminist Thought*, Patricia Hill Collins describes the stereotypes that uniquely affect African American women. She traces several stereotypes she saw as excluded from (white) feminism—including The Mammy, a servant figure; The Matriarch, an assertive (and therefore unfeminine) ruler of her family; The Welfare Mother, a passive baby-making machine; and The Jezebel, a sexually aggressive and sexually available black woman—back to tropes used to justify slavery.

However, (white) feminists including these racialized sexist tropes in their fight against patriarchy didn't go down well with Collins either. She writes in a 1993 essay:

> The longstanding effort to "colorize" feminist theory by inserting the experiences of women of color represents at best genuine efforts to reduce bias in Women's Studies. But at its worst, colorization also contains elements of both voyeurism and academic colonialism.

In the "increasingly sophisticated" new Theory, it seems impossible to do anything right. The needle Collins expects (white) feminists to thread involves including, but not appropriating, the experiences of women of color, providing space for them to be heard, and amplifying their voices—without exploiting them or becoming voyeuristic consumers of their oppression. These kinds of impossible, contradictory, double-bind demands are a persistent feature of applied postmodern Theory and continue to plague gender studies and other forms of Critical Social Justice scholarship. Rather than seeing these double-bind or no-win demands as a problem, however, Theorists tend to rely on them to assert their own moral authority and to insert themselves into positions of power (an approach some might reasonably refer to as "bullying").

And that's just the issue of race. Similar problems arise from the application of queer Theory. As a result, attempts to include more lesbian, gay, bisexual, and transgender voices in gender studies have often been met with frustration.

A Classless Theory

One more casualty of the "increasingly sophisticated" intersectional model is the neglect of the most materially relevant variable in many of the problems faced by women (and by many racial and sexual minorities): economic class. This neglect has gravely concerned left-leaning liberal feminists, socialist feminists, and socialists more broadly.

Privilege replaces class for intersectionalists. Privilege is a concept most closely associated with the Theorist Peggy McIntosh, author of a 1989 essay called "White Privilege: Unpacking the Invisible Knapsack," though she undoubtedly borrowed the idea from earlier discussions of "white-skin privilege" that precede her by decades. Although McIntosh, influenced by critical race Theory, focuses on *white* privilege, the concept of social privilege was soon extended to other identity categories—male, straight, cisgender, thin, able-bodied, and so on. The term describes the relative lack of discrimination and disenfranchisement people in these categories experience relative to those in marginalized identity categories. Thus, even if a light-skinned person doesn't gain specific benefits from their light skin, they at least don't experience the bad things they might face if they had dark skin.

Privilege in this sense isn't connected to economic class. Privilege-consciousness has nearly completely replaced class-consciousness as the primary concern of those on the academic, activist, and political left (under the name "engaging positionality"—exactly what Patricia Williams said is "everything" in her analysis of the law). A straight, white, cisgender male, even if he's poor, has, according to this logic, more privilege than a black, gay, transgender woman, no matter how rich she is. Traditional economic leftists find this shift away from class and toward gender identity, race, and sexuality troubling. They fear that the left is being taken away from the working class and hijacked by the bourgeoisie or elites within the academy. More worryingly still for those who care about social justice, this shift will drive working class voters into the arms of the far right.

New York University historian Linda Gordon has summarized working-class resentment of intersectionality:

> Some criticism is ill-informed but understandable, nevertheless. A poor white man associates intersectionality with being told that he has white privilege: "So when that feminist told me I had 'white privilege,' I told her that my white skin didn't do shit." He explains: "Have you ever spent a frigid northern-Illinois winter without heat or running water? I have. At 12 years old were you making ramen noodles in a coffee maker with water you fetched from a public bathroom? I was."

As intersectionality developed and became dominant in both mainstream political activism and scholarship, it became more common to hear that "straight, white, cisgendered men" are the problem. This is unlikely to make the left appeal to heterosexual white men—especially if they have experienced poverty, homelessness, or other major hardships.

Of Masculinities and Men

There is such a thing as "studies" of "men and masculinities" within gender studies, but this area of study doesn't seem likely to change the idea that men are the problem. The scholars of men's and masculinities studies are mostly men, but they study masculinity within a feminist framework. Put another way, feminism is the only lens permitted to study men and masculinity under Theory. Men speaking for themselves would be seen as speaking from power into dominant discourses, and women speaking for men would be seen as speaking into those same dominant discourses, so neither can be allowed.

Men's and masculinities studies often rely heavily on the concept of "hegemonic masculinity," developed by Australian gender Theorist Raewyn Connell. Hegemonic masculinity refers to dominant forms of masculinity, which maintain men's superiority over women and express maleness in aggressive and competitive ways, and which are socially enforced by hegemonic—dominant and powerful—discourses around what it means to be a "real man." Hegemonic masculinity is connected to the concept of "toxic masculinity," which was developed by psychiatrist Terry Kupers in his research on masculinity in prisons. He defines toxic masculinity as "the constellation of socially regressive male traits that serve to foster domination, the devaluation of women, homophobia, and wanton violence." As Theory has it, men are socialized into these performances of masculinity by a society that is structured by power dynamics that favor men and fail to question them.

Intersectionalism generally only redeems men when they also have some form of marginalized identity. For example, the "inclusive masculinity" developed by Eric Anderson in the mid-2000s was widely celebrated for its focus on homosexuality and feminism. There has been very little study of problems faced by men simply because they are men—outside of Theoretically sanctioned feminist, race, or sexuality issues.

Summary of the Shift

The shift toward intersectional feminism and gender studies can be summed up in these four ways:

1. Gender is highly significant to the way power is structured in society.

2. Gender is socially constructed.

3. Gendered power structures privilege men.

4. Gender is combined with other forms of identity, which must be acknowledged, and that knowledge is relative and attached to identity.

By the early 2000s, feminism had been almost completely swallowed up by gender studies. It largely abandoned its radical and materialist scholarly roots and liberal activism and replaced them with postmodern category blurring and cultural relativism—the effects of gender studies' heavy reliance on intersectionality and queer Theory and its intense emphasis on language. The focus on group identity and intersectional standpoint theory that now forms the backbone of Critical Social Justice thought leaves no room for the concepts of universality and individuality.

This analytical framework has some benefits. It upset the simplistic radical and materialist feminist metanarratives—in which women were an oppressed class and men their oppressors—by recognizing that power doesn't work in such a simple and binary way. This was particularly valuable to African American feminists, who were able to show that they faced very different stereotypes and barriers than white American feminists, and who expanded feminist scholarship to include them. It also encouraged the exploration of gender as something more complicated than roles imposed on men and women by patriarchy, by incorporating the prejudice and discrimination faced by trans men and women.

However, there have been a lot of problems with gender studies since its turn toward intersectionality. The current analytical framework doesn't allow for the possibility of a situation in which gender power imbalances *don't* exist or in which men are disadvantaged. It's often argued that "patriarchy harms men too," but intersectionalists refuse to consider that male dominance might not be a factor in every disparity. They also won't accept the argument that men could be systematically disadvantaged as a sex—say, for instance, by the rising social prestige of intersectional feminism.

Another problem is that not all gender differences can be explained by social constructivism or understood by Critical Theory. On average, women and men make different life choices, display different degrees of psychological traits, have different interests, and exhibit different sexual behaviors, but there is considerable evidence that much of this is because men and women are not innately psychologically identical. Social constructivists refuse to consider biological explanations for these differences on average. This limits their ability to do rigorous and valuable scholarship, while undermining the credibility of any rigorous and valuable scholarship that has been done in the field.

Finally, making all analyses of gender intersectional, focusing relentlessly on a simplistic concept of societal privilege rooted overwhelmingly in identity (and not in economics), and incorporating elements of critical race Theory and queer Theory, results in highly muddled scholarship. It becomes almost impossible to reach any conclusion other than the over-simplification that straight white men are unfairly privileged and need to repent and get out of everyone else's way. Indeed, because of this focus on identity and the perceived need for more scholars to have many different marginalized identities, large sections of academic papers are dedicated to scholars performatively acknowledging their positionality and problematizing their own work, rather than doing something useful to help heal the remaining divides between the genders.

This is the price it pays for its "increasing sophistication."

7 DISABILITY AND FAT STUDIES
Replacing Science with Wishful Thinking

As with gender studies, critical race Theory, and queer Theory, critical approaches to studying disability and fatness as identities began with the applied postmodern turn of the late 1980s and early 1990s. This led to the creation of disability studies and fat studies. In parallel to what happened in gender studies, these new areas of study have largely pushed out more practical approaches, which are less likely to believe everything is a social construct and best approached with identity politics.

Though similar in many respects, these two fields have different histories, so we'll talk about them separately.

Disability Studies

Disabled activism began in the 1960s, around the same time as the Civil Rights Movement, second-wave feminism, and Gay Pride. It aimed to make society more accommodating and accepting of disabled people, thereby improving their quality of life. Its activists wanted to increase disabled people's access to the opportunities available to the nondisabled, and the movement enjoyed some great success.

But disability studies began to change in the 1980s. After the turn toward applied postmodernism and the incorporation of intersectional feminism, queer Theory, and critical race Theory, disability studies began to view ability and disability as a social construct. Since then, it's become increasingly radical—and postmodern. Disability (including certain treatable mental illnesses) came to be valorized as a marginalized identity, and it was seen as unfairly devalued in relation to "normal" able-bodied identities. As a result, disability studies has taken an increasingly abstract approach, which makes it unsuited to the job of improving the opportunities and quality of life of disabled people.

"Dis/abled" (this strange term means the study of both the disabled and the abled) scholarship and activism in the 1980s shifted from understanding disability as something related to the individual, to viewing it as something imposed upon individuals by a society that doesn't accommodate their needs.

Before this shift, disabled people were seen as people whose disabilities affect the way they interact with the world. Afterward, disability was viewed as a status imposed upon them by an unwelcoming and uninterested society. For example, a person with deafness was previously considered to be a person who can't hear, who is disabled by the fact of her impairment. After the shift, she was seen as a Deaf person, someone who can't hear and whom society has "disabled" by failing to accommodate her as well as it has those who can hear. "Disabled" turns from being an adjective to describe an aspect of a person, to being something that has been done to a person (by the system). "I *am* disabled" becomes "I have *been* disabled (by society)."

In other words, a person is only disabled because of *society's assumption* that people are all able-bodied, and if society were to change radically enough, that person would not be disabled any longer.

This shift seems to have taken place in two stages. In the first, what is commonly called the "social model of disability" replaced the "medical model of disability," sometimes called the "individual" model. This occurred in the 1980s and is widely credited to the British social work scholar and sociologist Michael Oliver. Within the medical model, disability is something that affects a person, and the solution is to fix the disabling condition or relieve impairments, so that disabled people can either engage with the world more like able-bodied people do or accept that they can't engage with it. In the social model of disability, however, it's society that has disabled a person by failing to create environments that accommodate individuals with impairments.

Oliver created a shift of responsibility. The understanding of disability that existed in the 1980s, in Britain in particular, changed from one that expected disabled people to work out their own solutions to accessing all that society has to offer or accept being excluded from it to one that placed the responsibility for enabling greater access for disabled people onto society. This conceptual shift requires that society adjust to be accommodating of people with a wider range of physical abilities, not the other way around. This was a largely positive approach that helped disabled people engage more fully in society.

There's no evidence that Oliver himself took a postmodernist approach at the time. His advocacy of accommodating disability demanded much practically difficult social change, but his views were not radically socially constructivist about the nature of disability. However, his classic book, *Social Work with Disabled People*, cowritten with Bob Sapey and first published in 1983, has undergone development. Currently in its fourth edition with a third credited author, it now includes references to identity studies. For example, in the most recent edition, published in 2012, the language has clearly been influenced by intersectionality:

> [E]xperiences will undoubtedly be culturally located and reflect differences of class, race, gender and so forth, and so discourse may well be culturally biased. When using the social model, understanding also comes from recognising that historically experiences of disability have been culturally located in responses to impairment. The social model can be used by those in different cultures and within ethnic, queer or gender studies to illustrate disability in those situations. Equally these disciplines all need to take account of disableism with their communities.

This second stage of disability studies relies strongly on the two postmodern principles: knowledge as social construct and society consisting of systems of power and privilege. Disability studies now frequently draws on critical race Theory and relies heavily on both Michel Foucault and Judith Butler. It also frequently uses the postmodern themes of boundary blurring and the importance of discourse—accompanied by a radical distrust of science. This is a shift from a liberal position—that society should recognise that some people are disabled and accommodate their extra needs—to a postmodern position—that disability and ability are themselves oppressive social constructs that need to be dismantled. The concept of the individual is also criticized in this second stage of disability studies, due to the belief that individualism enables a "neoliberal expectation" that people should overcome their disabilities to become productive members of society for the benefit of capitalism rather than for their own fulfillment of potential.

Ableism

In current disability studies, "ableism" is the acceptance of the idea that it's better to be able-bodied than disabled and that being able-bodied is "normal." "Disableism," on the other hand, is prejudice against disabled people, including the idea that their disability is "abnormal" and the belief that an able-bodied person is superior to a disabled person.

Accordingly, queer Theory, with its focus on deconstructing the normal, works well with disability studies. Queer Theorist Judith Butler incorporated Adrienne Rich's concept of "compulsory heterosexuality"—the social enforcement of heterosexuality as the normal, default sexuality—and Robert

McRuer does the same in disability studies. In his 2006 book, *Crip Theory: Cultural Signs of Queerness and Disability*, which examines how queer Theory and disability studies inform each other, he argues,

> Like compulsory heterosexuality, then, compulsory able-bodiedness functions by covering over, with the appearance of choice, a system in which there is actually no choice. . . . Just as the origins of heterosexual/homosexual identity are now obscured for most people so that compulsory hetero-sexuality functions as a disciplinary formation seemingly emanating from everywhere and nowhere, so too are the origins of able-bodied/disabled obscured . . . to cohere in a system of compulsory able-bodiedness that similarly ema-nates from everywhere and nowhere.

This passage echoes Foucault's argument that different sex-ualities and mental illness were merely constructs of medical discourses that unjustly tried to categorize people as "normal" and "abnormal" and to exclude the "abnormal" from participa-tion in the dominant discourses of society. The view of ability status as something that is unjustly constructed as "normal" (able-bodied) or "abnormal" (disabled) has dominated disabil-ity studies ever since it adopted queer Theory's approaches.

In his 2014 book, *Disability Studies: Theorising Disableism and Ableism*, Dan Goodley uses this postmodern approach. He applies Foucault's concept of "biopower," in which scientific discourses have high prestige and are accepted as truth and perpetuated through society, where they create the categories they seem to describe. Goodley's use of the postmodern knowledge and political principles—he sees scientific discourses as oppressive and no more true than other ways of knowing—is clear when he compares science to colonialism:

> We know that colonial knowledges are constructed as neutral and universal through the mobilisation of associated discourses such as humanitarian, philanthropic and poverty alleviation measures. We might also ask: how are ableist knowledges naturalised, neutralised and universalised?

Goodley sees diagnosing, treating, and curing disabilities as suspicious practices that uphold ableist ideas and contribute to a "neoliberal system" in which people are forced to be fully autonomous, high-functioning individuals so they can contribute their labor to capitalist markets. Even more worryingly, he claims that "autonomy, independence, and rationality are virtues desired by neoliberal-ableism."

The postmodern political principle, which sees the world as constructed of systems of power, pervades Goodley's book. He describes society as "merging overlapping discourses of privilege" and writes,

> I argue that modes of ableist cultural reproduction and disabling material conditions can never be divorced from hetero/sexism, racism, homophobia, colonialism, imperialism, patriarchy and capitalism.

For Goodley, Oliver's social model isn't intersectional enough: it doesn't analyze race and gender and it doesn't see disability in queer Theory terms—as "an identity that might be celebrated as it disrupts norms and subverts values of society."

This idea that disabled people have a responsibility to use their disabilities to subvert social norms and categories—and even refuse any attempts at treatment or cure—is a common feature of disability studies. It appears in Fiona Campbell's 2009 book, *Contours of Ableism: The Production of Disability and Abledness.* Like Goodley, Campbell sees it as problematic that disabilities are seen as problems to be cured.

Within scholarship and activism, the wish to prevent or cure disability is often caricatured as wishing *disabled people* (rather than their disabilities) didn't exist. Campbell goes even further. Drawing on the queer Theory of Judith Butler, she characterizes able-bodiedness and disability as performances that people learn from society:

> Whether it be the "species typical body" (in science), the "normative citizen" (in political theory), the "reasonable man" (in law), all these signifiers point to a fabrication that reaches into the very soul that sweeps us into life and as such is the outcome and instrument of a political constitution. The creation of such regimes of ontological separation appears disassociated from power. . . . Daily the identities of *disabled* and *abled* are performed repeatedly.

This provocative passage not only includes Butler's idea of *performativity,* but it is also clearly influenced by Derrida. A Derridean's view would say that we understand "disability" and "able-bodiedness" only in their difference from each other, and the two concepts are not viewed equitably.

Campbell also incorporates critical race Theory, especially its tenet that racism is such a normal, ordinary, and natural part of Western life that no one sees or questions it. She adapts this to disability studies to argue that ableism is also such an ordinary form of prejudice that we don't question why we believe it's better to be able-bodied than to have an impairment. She even criticizes disabled people for having "internalized ableism" if they express any wish not to be disabled. She writes, "By unwittingly performing ableism, disabled people become complicit in their own demise, reinforcing impairment as an undesirable state."

These ideas are fairly typical of disability studies. Lydia X. Z. Brown, for example, also depicts disability as a performance and having a disability as an identity to be celebrated. This is apparent in Brown's account of a discussion with a Muslim convert friend, who had explained to Brown why she wears hijab, even though she doesn't believe in the modesty concept behind it:

> Wearing hijab is an outward sign of being Muslim. She was performing "being Muslim" and wanted to be associated with being Muslim, and chooses to wear the hijab so that other people—Muslim or not—can identify her, similarly to how I, as an Autistic person who doesn't instinctually or innately flap my hands or arms—it was never a stim that I developed independently—will deliberately and frequently choose to flap, especially in public, in order to call attention to myself, so that other people—whether autistic or not— might identify me as autistic. I use this as an outward sign,

[similar to how some Muslim women might choose to wear hijab even in the absence of religious convictions about head coverings].

This open attention-seeking performance probably wouldn't be appreciated by most autistic people. Still, some activists insist that their disabilities—including treatable mental illnesses, like depression, anxiety, and even being suicidal—are positives and compare them to other empowering aspects of identity.

For instance, in his book *No Pity: People with Disabilities Forming a New Civil Rights Movement*, Joseph Shapiro objects to the idea that it's a compliment when an able-bodied person doesn't think of a disabled person as disabled. He writes,

> It was as if someone had tried to compliment a black man by saying "You're the least black person I ever met," as false as telling a Jew, "I never think of you as Jewish," as clumsy as seeking to flatter a woman with "You don't act like a woman."

Shapiro likens Disabled Pride to Gay Pride. Having a disability, he feels, should be seen as a positive:

> Like homosexuals in the early 1970s, many disabled people are rejecting the "stigma" that there is something sad or to be ashamed of in their condition. They are taking pride in their identity as disabled people, parading it instead of closeting it.

This politicized approach is different from someone accepting their impairments and embracing their reality in a psychologically positive way. No one should be made to feel ashamed of their sexuality, race, religion, gender, or ability status, but many disabled people probably disagree with the view that their disability should be celebrated—and this view isn't likely to help in finding an effective treatment or remedy, if that's what they want. Wanting treatment and remedies isn't wrong, and not something to feel ashamed of.

The postmodern knowledge principle, which rejects the idea that doctors are any more qualified to diagnose disability than anyone else, often encourages people to self-diagnose, for the purpose of belonging to an identity group. A documented conversation between Lydia X. Z. Brown and Jennifer Scuro provides an example (LB and JS, respectively):

> LB: People do say to me, "I think I'm Autistic but I don't really want to say that because I've never been diagnosed," that is, given a diagnosis by someone with letters after their name. My response is: "Well, it's not up to me to tell you how you should or should not identify," but I don't believe in giving power to the medical-industrial complex and its monopoly over getting to define and determine who counts and who does not count as Autistic . . .

> JS: Yes, once I started to get into the territory of diagnosis, once I started playing around with the problem of diagnostic thinking when it is only left to trained diagnosticians, this allowed me to challenge how all of us must contend with thinking diagnostically.

This exchange seems to advocate that people self-identify as disabled for the purposes of gaining a group identity, disrupting medical science, and disrupting the dominant belief, in a politically motivated way, that disability is a thing to be avoided or treated.

It's unclear how any of this is helpful to disabled people.

Helpful Advocacy Derailed

Disability studies, activism, and the social model of disability started off well. Their initial goals were to lessen the burden on disabled people to adapt themselves to society and make society accommodate them and their disabilities better. This change of emphasis has been incorporated into various laws, and increased disabled people's access to employment and social opportunities they used to be barred from. It was fitting that scholarship should continue this work by studying social attitudes toward disability and trying to improve them.

Unfortunately, the incorporation of applied postmodern Theory into disability studies scholarship seems to have derailed it. This identity-obsessed approach pressures disabled people to identify with, celebrate, and politicize their disabilities. While disabled people can be constrained by medical labels, a deep suspicion of medical science in itself won't benefit disabled people or anyone else. Intersectionality is likely to unnecessarily complicate the issue of prejudice against the disabled by burying it under a mountain of "overlapping discourses of privilege." The use of critical race Theory's framework to insist that disabilities are ultimately social constructions is unhelpful, because physical and mental impairments are objectively real and people often dislike having them because of the way they negatively affect their lives (and not because they have been socialized to believe they should dislike them).

It's unethical to demand that disabled people take on their disability as an identity in order to disrupt ableist cultural norms. While some disabled people may find comfort and empowerment in identifying with their disability, many won't. Many disabled people wish they weren't disabled and want to improve their condition for themselves and others. (That is, in fact, the position of one of the authors of this book, who would prefer not to be in pain and limited in her movement and vision.) This is their right, and good disability activism should support it. Accusing those who want this of having "internalized ableism" is presumptuous and insulting.

One problem with taking on a physical or mental disability as an identity is that it turns any possible treatment of the disability into an act of erasure. This might lead people to problematize or refuse technology that, for example, allows deaf people to hear, because they won't be deaf afterward. Most deaf people whose hearing impairment could be improved by a hearing aid wouldn't reject that intervention, and it would be cruel to call them identity-traitors for taking it.

Disability studies and activism don't speak for all disabled people, and they could even hurt disabled people's ability to get the diagnoses and treatments they want. The status involved in having a marginalized identity may even produce an increased temptation to become more rather than less disabled and to focus overwhelmingly on one's disability. This is especially troubling if people can self-identify as disabled without a professional diagnosis or medical care.

Disability studies is well-intentioned, but ultimately it is a failure.

Fat Studies

Many of the same problems in disability studies appear in fat studies as well. Like disability studies, fat studies began in the United States in the 1960s, as fat activism, and has appeared in many forms since. It has only recently established itself as a distinct branch of identity studies. It also draws strongly on queer Theory and feminism and has a strongly intersectional focus. It attempts to portray negative perceptions of obesity as akin to racism, sexism, and homophobia, and it explicitly rejects science. It focuses on the social construction of obesity and seeks to empower obese people to reject medical advice and embrace a supportive community "knowledge" that sees obesity as a good thing.

Fat studies relies strongly on the postmodern knowledge principle, which sees knowledge as a construct of power, perpetuated in discourses—here, discourses rooted in *fatphobia*, combined with misogyny and racism. Fat studies creates highly complex frameworks of oppression, with a radical skepticism of science, and advocates "other ways of knowing," which include personal experiences, Theory, feminism, and even poetry.

It's most popular in the United Kingdom, but fat activism probably began in the United States, with the founding of the

National Association to Advance Fat Acceptance (NAAFA) in 1969 and the development of the Fat Underground in the 1970s. Fat activism came about within the set of social, cultural, and political changes that began to elevate cultural and identity studies, and postmodernism, in around the 1970s.

However, fat activism seems to have taken on postmodern traits much more recently than the other types of identity studies that rely on applied postmodern Theory. This is probably because fat studies didn't become a scholarly field until quite recently, though feminist scholars had long Theorized about pressure on women to be thin. Fat studies insists that pervasive and societally accepted "fatphobia" prevented it from being taken seriously and sees any study of obesity as a dangerous and (usually) treatable medical condition as fatphobic.

Historically, the scholarship and activism that became fat studies was called fat feminism. This was strongly associated with the radical and radical lesbian branches of feminism and had a limited following. This didn't change much until the 1990s, when the body positivity movement, which focused on acceptance and celebration of "fat bodies," emerged in the broader liberal society. A related Health at Every Size movement, which has existed in various forms since the 1960s, became prominent in 2003 when the Association for Size Diversity and Health trademarked the phrase. In 2010, Lindo Bacon (formerly Linda), a scholar of physiology and psychotherapy, wrote a popular book called *Health at Every Size: The Surprising Truth about Your Weight*, which argues that bodies of all sizes and dimensions can be healthy. Medical doctors disagree.

Fat studies developed rapidly, began taking on an applied postmodern approach, and soon became thoroughly intersectional. Fat studies' claim to be an independent discipline was strengthened in 2012, when the scholarly journal *Fat Studies* was founded. The journal explicitly compares negative opinions about obesity—including concerns about possible health implications of being overweight or obese—to prejudice against people for immutable characteristics.

Queer Theory and Judith Butler strongly influenced the development of fat studies. Leading fat scholar Charlotte Cooper begins her book *Fat Activism: A Radical Social Movement,* by declaring it to be "openly queer" and by "encouraging fat activists to resist the pull of access and assimilation, if they can, and consider queer strategies to reinvigorate the movement."

Foucault's concept of "biopower"—where science is seen as an unfairly privileged method of knowledge production, which is then perpetuated at all levels of society by discourse—is also used, in a rather paranoid way. This belief in hidden powerful discourses runs through fat activism texts at all levels and calls upon both Foucault and Butler. For fat scholar Marilyn Wann,

> Every person who lives in a fat-hating culture inevitably absorbs anti-fat beliefs, assumptions, and stereotypes, and also inevitably comes to occupy a position in relation to power arrangements that are based on weight. None of us can ever hope to be completely free of such training or completely disentangled from the power grid.

This is the way applied postmodernists see human society. They say elements of our identity position us on this grid with different levels of access to power. We learn to "perform" our position, conducting the power through ourselves as part of the system, often without even knowing that the grid is there. By performing our roles, we uphold the social and cultural assumptions that grant and deny access to power. We socialize ourselves and others into accepting the inequities of the system, justifying our own access and rationalizing the exclusion of others.

This is all done through discourses—ways we speak about things and how we represent them in nonverbal media. As this postmodern conception of society has evolved, it has consolidated into a belief system that the first postmodernists would never have agreed with.

Theory—A Paranoid Fantasy

For some fat studies scholars, fatphobia boils down to sexism. For others, it's capitalism. For Charlotte Cooper, for instance, the forces of "neoliberalism" (market-driven capitalist society) pressure people to adapt themselves to society, instead of requiring society to accommodate them. Cooper is deeply critical of the body positivity movement. She thinks that body positivity places all the responsibility on individuals to love their own bodies and be happy in them, instead of requiring society to stop viewing obesity negatively. As Liz, a member of Cooper's "fat community" whom Cooper interviewed for *Fat Activism,* argues, "Fat hatred is fuelled by capitalism because these companies create products that are all about making fat people skinny."

Biology and the science of nutrition are misunderstood as a form of Foucauldian "biopower," which constrains and disciplines people. Medical science around obesity is misunderstood as an oppressive, disciplinary force oppressing obese people. In the foreword to *The Fat Studies Reader,* Marilyn Wann tells us that "calling fat people 'obese' medicalizes human diversity" and that "[m]edicalizing diversity inspires a misplaced search for a 'cure' for naturally occurring difference." This echoes Foucault. Kathleen LeBesco compares obesity to homosexuality—a naturally occurring phenomenon that doesn't need a cure.

Despite the evidence that obesity increases the risk of serious diseases and early death, LeBesco also speculates that obese people who think their weight is a problem have been conditioned into accepting their oppression:

> That fat and queer people would heartily embrace science and medicine as a solution to their socially constructed problems is redolent of Stockholm syndrome—after all, science and medicine have long been instrumental in oppressing fat and queer people, providing argument after argument that pathologize the homosexual or "obese" individual (whether the mind or the body).

Emphasizing the value of health is cast as a problematic ideology called *healthism*. Healthism is bolstered by *nutritionism*, which is an allegedly excessive focus on the relevance of the nutritional value of foods and their impact on health.

There are also "critical" fields of dietetics and nutrition studies, which are about Critical Social Justice, not diet and nutrition. Rather than using science to understand diet and nutrition and their health implications, critical dieticians "have instead chosen to engage poetry as a way of 'crafting a praxis-oriented culture' and troubling the status quo." They urge a "re-think of how dietetic attitudes toward fatness and gender play a role in legitimating and constructing science."

While the Health at Every Size approach stopped short of denying medical science and instead interpreted medical stud-ies to claim one can be healthy at any weight, the book *Critical Dietetics and Critical Nutrition Studies* describes science as no more useful than any other approach to understanding food, nutrition, diet, and fatness:

> Although we do not wholly reject the scientific method as a means of creating knowledge about the world, a critical ori-entation rejects the notion that it is even possible to produce knowledge that is objective, value-free, and untouched by human bias. A critical orientation similarly rejects the idea that any one way of creating knowledge about the world is superior to another or is even sufficient. . . . As such, [critical dietetics] draws on post-structuralism and feminist science (two other windows) that hold that there is not one truth that can be generated about any single thing, that multiple truths are possible depending on who is asking and for what purpose, and that knowledge is not apolitical even if it is considered positivist (i.e. value neutral or unbiased).

This is an explicit rejection of objective reality. "Post-structuralism and feminist science" are used to dismiss the overwhelming evidence that nutrition plays a significant role in health and that obesity increases the risk of heart disease, several cancers, and diabetes—not to mention polycystic ovary syndrome, joint problems, mobility problems, and respiratory problems—and is strongly correlated with early death. This health denialism is the approach taken by Cooper too. She advocates "research justice," in which empirical studies of obesity can be swapped out at will for "embodied community knowledge" in order to "unlock knowledge that has already been generated by fat people."

Support-Group Scholarship

Fat studies and fat activism seem to have started in various places at different times and have many strands. In addition to its radical lesbian feminist origins, fat activism includes a celebratory body positivity movement, a dubious but popular Health at Every Size campaign, and (recently) an intersectional queer feminist branch with its own Theory.

The popularity of these approaches suggests there's a need for some kind of advocacy and community for obese people. Fat activism could have a valuable role to play in society, if it could counter discrimination and prejudice against obese people and provide a support network, without descending into radical social constructivism, paranoia, and science denial.

Sadly, fat studies is currently among the most irrational and ideological forms of scholarship-activism in identity studies. A latecomer to the party, it has incorporated so many existing forms of identity-driven Theory that it doesn't really have an internally consistent framework of its own. It's messy and confusing, veering from critical race to feminist to queer Theory, while weaving in anticapitalist rhetoric and ideas taken from disability studies. Fat studies tries to associate itself with forms of activism and scholarship that address prejudice against people on the grounds of immutable characteristics like race, sex, and sexuality, but it ignores the evidence that obesity isn't usually immutable: it's a result of overeating.

A productive form of fat activism could work against the idea that overeating is simply the result of a lack of self-discipline or of greed and look at the psychological and physiological issues that make this problem hard to overcome for so many people—but this isn't the approach fat studies takes. Instead, it adopts the postmodern knowledge and political principles and applies the four postmodern themes in an approach that resembles more of a support group than a rigorous academic discipline.

Fat activism can also be criticized for undermining other forms of activism by trying to claim kinship with them. The idea that obesity is just like homosexuality, for example, could threaten the newly commonplace view that homosexuality is natural and perfectly healthy. It's also clearly unfair to accuse obese people of Stockholm syndrome or internalized fatphobia if they're unhappy being overweight.

Above all other criticism, though, is the fact that this form of fat activism is potentially dangerous. People who have difficulty managing their weight and suffer from low self-esteem as a result can be encouraged to reject the medical evidence that obesity is a serious health problem. If fat activism reaches the same status as feminist and antiracist activism, doctors, scientists, and researchers could feel hesitant to give patients factual medical information about obesity, and as a result, obese individuals wouldn't be able to make informed choices about their health.

Fat studies has found a home within the various fields of study that might collectively be called *Critical Social Justice scholarship*. These fields vary widely, though they have enough in common to be readily identifiable: they are usually called "critical X" or "X studies," where X is whatever they want to complain about, disrupt, and modify, using Critical Theory and the postmodern knowledge and political principles (critical constructivism, i.e., applied postmodernism). Despite addressing a range of concerns, which encompass almost all human endeavors, they share one common element: a form of Theory that treats the underlying postmodern assumptions as *objectively real*.

We now turn our attention to this.

8 CRITICAL SOCIAL JUSTICE SCHOLARSHIP AND THOUGHT
Making Theory True

In the first phase of postmodernism (roughly 1965–1990), the postmodern knowledge principle and the postmodern political principle were used solely to deconstruct. In the second phase (1990–2010), they were turned into applied postmodernism, and postmodernism fragmented into postcolonial Theory, queer Theory, critical race Theory, intersectional feminism, disability studies, and fat studies.

Since 2010, after decades of growth and development in academia and activism, the principles, themes, and assertions of Theory became *known-knowns*—ideas taken for granted as true statements about the world. Society being made up of specific but invisible identity-based systems of power and privilege that construct knowledge via discourse is now considered by Critical Social Justice scholars and activists to be an objectively true statement about society.

Kind of sounds like a metanarrative, doesn't it?

That's because it is. The original postmodern doubt that any knowledge can be reliable has been gradually transformed into complete certainty that knowledge is constructed in the service of power, which is rooted in identity, and that this can be uncovered through close readings of how we use language. Critical Social Justice scholarship continually talks about how patriarchy, white supremacy, imperialism, cisnormativity, heteronormativity, ableism, and fatphobia are literally structuring society and infecting everything. They are always present, just beneath the surface. They need to be constantly identified, condemned, and dismantled so that we can fix them.

Critical Social Justice texts—which form a kind of Gospel of Critical Social Justice—express, with absolute certainty, that all white people are racist, all men are sexist, racism and sexism are systems that can exist and oppress without even a single person with racist or sexist intentions, sex is not biological and exists on a spectrum, language can be literal violence, denial of gender identity is killing people, the wish to remedy disability and obesity is hateful, and everything needs to be decolonized.

This approach distrusts categories and boundaries and seeks to blur them. It's intensely focused on language as a means of creating and perpetuating power imbalances. It exhibits a deep cultural relativism, focuses on marginalized groups, and has little time for universal principles or individual intellectual diversity. These are the four themes of postmodernism, and they're central to the means and ethics of Critical Social

Justice scholarship. In the new Critical Social Justice scholarship, Theory's principles and themes have become much simpler and much more straightforward, because they've been *reified*—made concrete and real.

Critical Social Justice scholarship doesn't neatly fit into any one category of Theory. It uses all of the principles and themes as needed, continually problematizing society and even aspects of itself, and abiding by only one golden rule: Theory itself can never be denied, because Theory is real. Critical Social Justice scholarship has become a kind of Theory of Everything, a set of unquestionable Truths with a capital T and the one true method for comprehending and acting upon them.

Postmodernism Evolving

As these Theories developed through the late 1990s into the 2000s, they became more intersectional. By the mid-2000s, if you studied one of the key topics—sex, gender identity, race, sexuality, immigration status, indigeneity, colonial status, disability, religion, or weight—you were expected to factor in all the others. While scholars could have particular focuses, there was a lot of mixing and merging. This resulted in a form of general scholarship that looks at "marginalized groups" and multiple systems of power and privilege.

As these marginalized groups united and the various streams of thought merged, Critical Social Justice scholars and activists also became much more confident in their ideas. As the 2010s began, postmodernism's signature ambiguity and doubt had almost entirely disappeared, and so had the dense, obscure language. By the 2010s, the language, while still technical, was far stronger. These were words of conviction.

Critical Social Justice uses identity as a lens through which to determine what is true. Consequently, a lot of the scholarship since 2010 is labeled "feminist," "queer," etc., *epistemology* (the study of the nature of knowledge) or *pedagogy* (the study of teaching methods). Nearly all Critical Social Justice scholarship is concerned with what is said, what is believed, what is assumed, what is taught, what is conveyed, and what biases are imported through teaching, discourses, and stereotypes.

All this scholarship begins with the idea that society is made up of systems of power and privilege that are maintained in language, and these systems create knowledge from the perspectives of the privileged and deny the perspectives of the marginalized.

A Menagerie of New Terms

When an ideology begins to solidify, its adherents realize they need to be able to prove that the ideology is based in reality. To do this, they develop systems of *epistemology*, theories of how knowledge is produced and understood.

For instance, feminist philosophy developed several epistemologies in the 1980s, most notably feminist empiricism, standpoint theory, and postmodern radical skepticism. Feminist empiricism says that science generally operates correctly except that, before feminism, it was full of bias toward males that prevented it from being objective. This method fell out of fashion in the 1990s. Standpoint theory and postmodern radical skepticism use the postmodern knowledge principle—that knowledge flows from identity—and today form the backbone of the intersectional approach to epistemology. Since 2010, they have also been mainstreamed throughout society.

In 2007, Miranda Fricker coined the term *epistemic injustice* in her book *Epistemic Injustice: Power and the Ethics of Knowing*. Epistemic injustice occurs when someone's capacity to know is insulted or doubted. According to Fricker, this can happen in a number of ways:

- When someone is not recognized as someone who *can* know something.

- When their knowledge is not recognized as valid.

- When they're prevented from being able to know something.

- When their knowledge is misunderstood.

Fricker divides epistemic injustice into *testimonial injustice*— when people are not considered credible because of their identity—and *hermeneutical injustice*—when someone's specialized knowledge can't be understood.

Fricker's analysis isn't totally wrong. People often do trust the knowledge of some individuals or groups more than others, and this may sometimes be due to social prejudices (e.g., racism) rather than to those people's actual degree of relevant expertise. Also, members of marginalized groups are sometimes alienated from knowledge related to their identity. For instance, lesbians and gay men in small communities in which homosexuality is not discussed may find it hard to understand their own sexuality, and atheists may struggle to comprehend their own lack of faith if they've never heard disbelief talked about openly before.

Fricker saw these as problems created and faced by *individuals*, rather than *groups*. Her individualistic approach didn't go down well with Critical Social Justice scholars, who criticized her for being overly simplistic and neglecting the need for widespread structural change. They have since drawn upon, expanded, and reoriented her work, depicting injustice as happening to social groups and caused by social power.

Fricker's work led to an explosion of new terms. In 2014, Kristie Dotson expanded and recontexualized Fricker's concept of epistemic injustice, which she sees as a superficial aspect of a bigger, identity-group-based problem she calls *epistemic oppression*. Dotson says this form of oppression occurs when the knowledges and knowledge-producing methods said to be used by marginalized groups are not included within our prevailing understanding of knowledge. Some scholars and activists have used this rationale to advocate factually inaccurate folk wisdom and witchcraft.

Dotson's work on epistemic oppression was a continuation of her earlier (2011) work on *epistemic violence*—having one's cultural knowledge repressed by that of a dominant culture. *Epistemic exploitation* was coined in 2010 by Nora Berenstain to describe the injustice caused when marginalized people are expected to share their knowledge. Thus, it can be considered an act of oppression not to make an effort to understand a marginalized knower on her own terms *and* an act of exploitation to ask a marginalized knower to explain her knowledge to you.

In 2013, José Medina coined the melodramatic term *hermeneutical death*, which describes a misunderstanding so profound that it destroys the person's sense of self. At the opposite end of this spectrum is the concept of *hermeneutical privacy*, which describes the right not to be understandable at all.

So, marginalized people can be oppressed to the point of psychic death by not being understood, but their right to be completely incomprehensible should also be respected. Again, we see the impossibility of getting it right.

Fricker's *testimonial injustice* has inspired a growing number of related ideas like *testimonial betrayal, epistemic freedom*, and *epistemic responsibility*. We could go on, but we think you get the idea—"knowledges" and demands for respect for those "knowledges" are the point of focus throughout Critical Social Justice scholarship.

Who You Are Is What You Know

Why the obsession with knowledges and knowers? To dodge more rigorous methods when objective reality stands between Critical Social Justice scholars and their ideological aims.

The problem, for them, is that scientific forms of knowledge production aim to be objective and universal, and (mostly) succeed. Because there are scientific explanations for some of the social issues that impact identity groups, science often finds itself in disagreement with the postmodern principles, especially the belief that everything important is socially constructed. In addition, many philosophers and scientists have identified flaws in Theory and in Critical Social Justice scholarship's assumptions, methods, and conclusions. Science and reason have an irritating habit of revealing the flaws in Theoretical approaches. They're *universal*, so they violate the postmodern knowledge principle and the postmodern theme of centering group identity, which Critical Social Justice organizes itself around.

Because science has such a high prestige as a reliable producer of knowledge—and because postmodernists from Lyotard to Foucault have disparaged it as a discourse of power for decades—Critical Social Justice scholars and activists are very suspicious of it. They rationalize this by pointing out that science and reason have historically been used to prop up injustices. Claims like this often refer to much earlier periods of science—citing, for example, nineteenth-century pseudoscientific arguments in support of colonialism that are now totally dismissed. They're also suspicious of science because it has discovered things that don't conform to social-constructivist ideas, such as differences between men and women.

Instead of science, Critical Social Justice scholarship often advocates for "other ways of knowing," derived from Theoretical interpretations of deeply felt lived experience. It argues that reason and evidence-based knowledge are *unfairly* favored over tradition, folklore, interpretation, and emotion because of the power imbalances baked into them. Theory views evidence and reason to be the cultural property of white Western men, ignoring how racist and sexist such a view is.

The concept of experiential knowledge isn't without merit. Quite often, it's more important to know how things are experienced than what the facts of the matter are. For example, if your friend's father dies of a heart attack, you would want to know how your friend is feeling and how you can help her through her grief rather than all the factual, medical information about heart attacks. There are important facts about heart attacks, and we need accurate information about them, but that knowledge can't be gained by experiencing a heart attack or losing a loved one to a heart attack. Sometimes we need to empathize with the person who has lost her loved one to a heart attack and sometimes we need to consult a cardiologist.

Despite postmodernists treating this idea as if it's new and profound, the divide between facts and experience is not particularly mysterious to philosophers outside of postmodernism: it's the difference between knowing *that* and knowing *how*. "Knowing that" is propositional knowledge, while "knowing how" is experiential knowledge. The trouble is not that this divide exists or that there's valuable information on both sides of it. The problems arise when we fail to recognize that interpretation colors, biases, and distorts experiential knowledge—at times profoundly—and makes it an unreliable guide to understanding the associated phenomena.

This confusion forms the basis of the argument of another Critical Social Justice Theorist, Alexis Shotwell, who argues that "focusing on propositional knowledge as though it is the only form of knowing worth considering is itself a form of epistemic injustice. Such a focus neglects epistemic resources that help oppressed people craft more just worlds."

Shotwell's commitment to the postmodern principles is confirmed when she writes, "A richer account of forms of knowing and a richer attention to people's lived experiences in the world helps us identify, analyze, and redress epistemic injustices." This is *standpoint theory*.

A Different Kind of Colorblindness

Standpoint theory operates on two assumptions. One is that people with the same marginalized identity—race, gender, sex, sexuality, ability status, and so on—will have similar experiences of dominance and oppression and will interpret them in the same ways. The other is that one's position within a social power dynamic ("positionality") dictates what one can and can't know. The privileged are blinded by their privilege and the oppressed possess a kind of double sight, because they understand both the dominant position and the experience of being oppressed by it.

Roughly, the idea is that members of oppressed groups understand the dominant perspective *and* the perspective of the oppressed, while members of dominant groups understand only the dominant perspective. Standpoint theory can be compared to a kind of colorblindness—the more privileged a person is, the fewer colors she can see. A straight white male might see only shades of gray. A black person would also be able to see shades of red, a woman would be able to see shades of green, and an LGBT person would be able to see shades of blue. A black lesbian would be able to see all three colors, in addition to the grayscale vision everyone has. The oppressed are thought to have a richer, more accurate view of reality, so we should listen to and believe their accounts of it.

Standpoint theory often finds itself criticized for essentialism—for saying something like, "All black people feel like this." Critical Social Justice scholars get around this accusation by arguing that the theory does not assume all members of the same group *have the same nature* but that *they experience the same problems in an unjust society* (sometimes called "structural determinism"). Members of these groups who disagree with standpoint theory—or even deny that they're oppressed—are said to have internalized their oppression ("false consciousness") or to be pandering in order to gain favor or reward from the dominant system ("Uncle Toms" and "native informants") by amplifying dominant discourses.

In other words, legitimate disagreement is not an option.

Thou Shalt Not Disagree with Theory

One of the most worrying things about Critical Social Justice scholarship is that disagreement is rarely tolerated. At best, disagreement is often seen as failure to engage with the scholarship correctly—as though if you had, you would surely agree—and, at worst, a profound moral failure. Religious ideology works in a similar way: if you don't believe, you haven't read the holy text properly or you just want to sin.

Caring about justice in society isn't the problem—indeed, it's necessary. It's also not inherently a problem if bad ideas gain popularity in academia. Afterall, knowledge advances when our centers of learning give space to all kinds of ideas, so they can be examined, tested, and criticized. Some of the most well-established ideas of today—like the "Big Bang" theory of cosmology—were considered crazy and unethical at one time.

But it is a problem when a school of thought refuses to submit its ideas to scrutiny, rejects any kind of examination on principle, and asserts that any attempts to subject it to thoughtful criticism are immoral, insincere, and proof that it's correct.

To get a better sense of this problem, let's look at three examples of Critical Social Justice scholarship from the 2010s.

Example 1: *Being White, Being Good: White Complicity, White Moral Responsibility, and Social Justice Pedagogy* by Barbara Applebaum (2010)

In this book, educator Barbara Applebaum argues that all white people are either racist or complicit in racism (usually both), because of their automatic participation in the system of power and privilege described by critical race Theory. Her book isn't well-known among the general public, but it's an exemplar in critical whiteness and critical education Theory circles because it advances the idea that all white people have white privilege (a concept that dates to 1989 and the applied postmodern turn) to insist that all white people are therefore actively complicit in racism. She writes,

> White students often assume that responsibility begins and ends with the awareness of privilege. By admitting to or con-

fessing privilege, however, white students are actually able to avoid owning up to their complicity in systemic racism.

This really does say that confessing to white privilege isn't enough. White students must accept that they are complicit in systemic racism simply because they're white. They have learned, internalized, and continually perpetuate racism even if they don't know it. She also remarks that this privilege cannot simply be renounced, or "checked."

If this reminds you of Foucault's notion of powerful discourses working through everyone in society, you're right. "Integral to the understanding of how discourse works," Applebaum writes, "is the Foucaultian notion of power." "Not only is discourse the prism through which reality is given meaning," she tells us, "but also power works through discourse to constitute subjects."

Again, we get this image of power working as a grid, through the people positioned on it, each performing and speaking according to its directives—rather like (nerd alert!) a Borg hive in *Star Trek*.

Applebaum demands people believe this paradigm, but she's quick to point out that she is not *technically* forbidding disagreement. She writes,

One can disagree and remain engaged in the material, for example, by asking questions and searching for clarification and understanding. Denials, however, function as a way to distance oneself from the material and to dismiss without engagement.

So, one can ask questions about Applebaum's thesis and try to understand it, but denial (what we usually think of as disagreement) can only mean one has not engaged with the material enough or in the right way.

In other words, Applebaum assumes that her thesis is true. She's certain that she is in possession of The Truth, and scolds those who disagree: "[T]he mere fact that they can question the existence of systemic oppression is a function of their privilege to choose to ignore discussions of systemic oppression or not." Applebaum doesn't seem to be remotely open to people disagreeing with her. Her students certainly appear to feel this way:

> [S]tudents in courses that make systemic injustice explicit often complain in teacher evaluations that they have not been allowed to disagree in the course. Students often maintain that such courses indoctrinate a particular view about racism that they are not willing to accept.

Applebaum says student disagreement like this should be shut down. She gives the example of a male student who questioned the gender wage gap:

> Allowing him to express his disagreement and spending time trying to challenge his beliefs often comes at a cost to marginalized students whose experiences are (even if indirectly) dismissed by his claims.

Critical education Theory believes it's dangerous to allow students to express such disagreement, because it believes that social reality and what is accepted as true are constructed by language—that's the postmodern knowledge principle. Disagreement would allow dominant discourses to be reasserted, voiced, and heard, which Theory sees as unsafe. As Applebaum explains, "language constitutes our reality by providing the conceptual framework from which meaning is given." She adds, "Even if one retreats to the position where one only speaks for oneself, one's speech is still not neutral and still reinforces the continuance of dominant discourses by omission."

Applebaum continues,

> Resistance will not be allowed to derail the class discussions! Of course, those who refuse to engage might mistakenly perceive this as a declaration that they will not be allowed to express their disagreement but that is only precisely *because* they are resisting engagement.

Like with *Star Trek*'s Borg, resistance is futile.

Example 2: "Tracking Privilege-Preserving Epistemic Pushback in Feminist and Critical Race Philosophy Classes" by Alison Bailey (2017)

In this essay, philosopher Alison Bailey argues that anyone who disagrees with Critical Social Justice scholarship is just trying to preserve unjust power structures, in the service of a knowledge-producing system that privileges straight white men and prevents Critical Social Justice. She also explicitly notes that the roots of her approach reject what is normally called "critical thinking" in favor of Critical Theory, which she explicitly identifies as "neo-Marxian" and proceeding from a set of assumptions that reject the critical-thinking approach in favor of power-based analysis.

She defines it like this: "Privilege-preserving epistemic pushback is a variety of willful ignorance that dominant groups habitually deploy during conversations that are trying to make social injustices visible." Criticism of Critical Social Justice work is immoral and harmful, Bailey tells us:

> I focus on these ground-holding responses because they are pervasive, tenacious, and bear a strong resemblance to critical-thinking practices, and because I believe that their uninterrupted circulation does psychological and epistemic harm to members of marginalized groups.

Since Bailey assumes that disagreement with her work must be a result of intellectual and moral failings, no disagreement can ever be tolerated:

> Treating privilege-preserving epistemic pushback as a form of critical engagement validates it and allows it to circulate more freely; this, as I'll argue later, can do epistemic violence to oppressed groups.

Bailey refers to disagreements with Critical Social Justice as "shadow texts," to suggest that written criticisms of Critical Social Justice aren't real scholarship. The image of *shadow texts*, she tells us, comes from the idea of an investigator shadowing her mark: "The word 'shadow' calls to mind the image of something walking closely alongside another thing without engaging it."

One example she gives of a shadow text involves a female student arguing that one can *mention* a racist slur in order to discuss it, without *using* it as a slur. Bailey responds,

> We are discussing institutional racism. Jennifer, a white philosophy major, shares a story about racist graffiti that uses the "n" word. She says the word, animating it with that two-fingered scare-quote gesture to signal that she is mentioning it. I ask her to consider the history of the word and how it might mean something different coming from white mouths. I ask her not to use it. She gives the class a mini lecture on the use–mention distinction, reminding me that it "is a foundational concept in analytic philosophy" and that it's "perfectly acceptable to mention, but not to use the word in philosophical discussions." . . . If Jennifer continues to press philosophical concepts into the service of a broader refusal to understand the dehumanizing history of the n-word, then "I mentioned but didn't use the word 'n-----'" is a shadow text.

Rather than consider the argument, Bailey assumes that Jennifer is trying to preserve white privilege. She then uses her as an example of failure to genuinely engage.

"Learning to spot shadow texts can offer epistemic friction: they help the class focus on what shadow texts do, rather than just on what they say," she writes. Bailey is instructing her philosophy classes not to engage with the argument students like Jennifer make, but to recognize which discourse of power they could be feeding into. Bailey teaches her philosophy classes to identify counterviews as resistance to Critical Social Justice and as a kind of "ignorance." She thinks that, when people disagree, it's because something "triggered the resistance." She adds,

> I ask our class to consider how identifying shadow texts might help track the production of ignorance. . . . It's essential for them to understand that tracking ignorance requires that our attention be focused not on a few problem individuals, but on learning to identify patterns of resistance and tying ignorance-producing habits to a strategic refusal to understand.

Like Applebaum, Bailey is certain of her own rightness and the need to reeducate and shut down anyone who disagrees. This marks a significant change from the earliest postmodernists' radical skepticism, but it's in keeping with how the postmodern principles and their application have evolved over the last half-century as they incorporated more and more Critical Theory.

Example 3: *White Fragility: Why It Is So Hard to Talk to White People about Race* by Robin DiAngelo (2018)

In this book, lecturer in "whiteness studies" Robin DiAngelo develops the concept of "white fragility" that she first laid out in a highly cited paper of that title from 2011. She begins that paper with a strong objective truth claim:

> White people in North America live in a social environment
> that protects and insulates them from race-based stress. This
> insulated environment of racial protection builds white ex-
> pectations for racial comfort while at the same time lower-
> ing the ability to tolerate racial stress, leading to what I refer
> to as White Fragility.

By itself this might be a useful insight, leading white people
to reflect more deeply about their possibly unconscious prejudices. But DiAngelo goes on to insist that society is permeated
by white supremacy and that any disagreement with her ideas
is the result of a weakness that has been socialized into white
people through their privilege:

> White Fragility is a state in which even a minimum amount
> of racial stress becomes intolerable, triggering a range of de-
> fensive moves. These moves include the outward display of
> emotions such as anger, fear, and guilt, and behaviors such
> as argumentation, silence, and leaving the stress-inducing
> situation.

Any negative feelings about being racially profiled and held
responsible for a racist society are taken as signs of being
"fragile." White people are complicit beneficiaries of racism
and white supremacy. Disagreement is not allowed. DiAngelo
is quite explicit about this saying that disagreeing, remaining
silent, and leaving the room are all evidence of fragility. The
only way to avoid being "fragile" is to remain seated, show no
negative emotions, and agree with The Truth—after which one
must actively learn how to deconstruct whiteness and white

privilege, which is billed as the necessary work of "antiracism."

DiAngelo, herself a white woman, says that all white people are racist and that it's impossible not to be, because of the systems of powerful racist discourses we were born into. She insists that we are complicit by default and responsible for addressing these systems.

In the book based on her paper, she argues that it doesn't matter if individual white people are good people who despise racism and are not aware of having any racist biases:

> Being good or bad is not relevant. Racism is a multilayered system embedded in our culture. All of us are socialized into the system of racism. Racism cannot be avoided. Whites have blind spots on racism, and I have blind spots on racism. Racism is complex, and I don't have to understand every nuance of the feedback to validate that feedback. Whites are / I am unconsciously invested in racism. Bias is implicit and unconscious.

DiAngelo writes as a white person addressing other white people, and insists "we" should see the world the way she does,

> This book is unapologetically rooted in identity politics. I am white and am addressing a common white dynamic. I am mainly writing to a white audience; when I use the terms us and we, I am referring to the white collective.

For Theorists like DiAngelo, white people are "socialized into a deeply internalized sense of superiority that we either are unaware of or can never admit to ourselves." All white people can do is become more aware of their relationship to power and consciously address it.

DiAngelo also rejects the liberal principles of individualism and "colorblindness"—that a person's race is irrelevant to her worth, as Martin Luther King, Jr. argued. According to Critical Social Justice, liberal values are racist because they enable white people to hide from the "realities" of their own racism and white supremacy. DiAngelo says,

> To challenge the ideologies of racism such as individualism and color blindness, we as white people must suspend our perception of ourselves as unique and/or outside race. Exploring our collective racial identity interrupts a key privilege of dominance—the ability to see oneself only as an individual.

DiAngelo's ideas, arguably more than any other, have successfully broken the bounds of academia and entered the mainstream. As of this writing, *White Fragility* has been on the *New York Times* bestseller list for nearly three years and has sold well over a million copies in the United States alone.

Making the Postmodern Principles and Themes Real

Critical Social Justice scholarship doesn't just rely on the two postmodern principles and four postmodern themes: it treats them as morally righteous capital-T Truth. Therefore, Critical Social Justice scholarship and activism make up a third distinct phase of postmodernism, one we call *reified postmodernism*, because it treats the abstract ideas of postmodernism as if they were real truths about society.

To understand how the three phases of postmodernism have developed, imagine a tree with deep roots in radical leftist social theory. The first phase, or *high deconstructive phase,* from the 1960s to the 1980s (usually just referred to as "postmodernism"), gave us the tree trunk: Theory. The second phase, from the 1980s to the mid-2000s, which we call *applied postmodernism,* gave us the branches—the more applicable Theories and studies, including postcolonial Theory, queer Theory, critical race Theory, gender studies, fat studies, disability studies, and many other "critical" studies. In the third phase, which began in the mid-2000s, Theory has gone from being an assumption to being The Truth. This gives us the leaves of the tree of Critical Social Justice scholarship, which combines the previous approaches as needed.

Critical Social Justice scholarship doesn't just play around with ideas like "objective truth doesn't exist" (the postmodern knowledge principle) and "society is constructed through language by discourses designed to keep the dominant in power over the oppressed" (the postmodern political principle), the way the earliest postmodernists did. It treats these ideas as The Truth and expects everyone to agree or be "cancelled." The four postmodern themes are also treated as facets of The Truth According to Critical Social Justice. The blurring of boundaries and cultural relativism typical of the applied postmodernist Theories have been developed further, and group identity is treated as so integral to the functioning of society that those invested in Critical Social Justice have elevated group-identity politics to a fever pitch.

Let's look at the contradiction at the heart of third-phase reified postmodernism: how can intelligent people be both radically skeptical and radical relativists, and at the same time argue for Critical Social Justice with such certainty?

The answer seems to be that the skepticism and relativism of the postmodern knowledge principle are now interpreted in a more restrictive way: it's thought to be impossible for humans to obtain reliable knowledge using evidence and reason, but reliable knowledge can be obtained by listening to the "lived experience" of members of marginalized groups—or, more accurately, to marginalized people's interpretations of their own lived experience, as long as they're properly colored by Theory.

But what should we do when different members of the same marginalized group—or members of different marginalized groups—give conflicting interpretations of their "lived experience"? The common-sense answer is that different people have different experiences and different interpretations, and that there is no logical contradiction in that, but that's incompatible with Critical Social Justice. Critical Social Justice epistemology claims that these "lived experiences" reveal objective truths about society, not merely some people's beliefs about their experiences.

Critical Social Justice scholars sometimes attempt the radically relativist answer—that two or more contradictory statements can be simultaneously true—but it doesn't make much sense. Instead, what they seem to do is select certain favored interpretations of marginalized people's experience (those consistent with Theory) and call these the "authentic" ones.

Dissenters are explained away as being self-interested or having internalized dominant ideologies.

This makes Critical Social Justice Theory completely unfalsifiable and, in philosophical terms, indefeasible. No matter what evidence about reality (physical, biological, and social) or philosophical argument might be presented, Theory always can and always does explain it away. This isn't very far from what we see with apocalyptic cults who predict that the world will end on a specific day but, instead of admitting they were wrong, invent stories to explain why their beliefs are still true when the day of the supposed apocalypse passes uneventfully—the spaceship coming to destroy the earth really *did* come, but the aliens changed their minds when they saw the cult members' devotion. Or something.

Unfortunately, Theory hasn't just stayed in universities. After becoming applied in the second phase, then reified in the third phase, postmodernism in the form of Critical Social Justice has left the universities, spread by graduates and through social media and activist journalism. It has become a significant cultural force with a huge—and often negative—influence on politics. It may seem like an obscure and peculiar brand of academic theorizing, but it can't be ignored.

What does all this mean? What will happen next? And what needs to be done about it? That's what the last two chapters of this book will address.

9 CRITICAL SOCIAL JUSTICE IN ACTION
Practicing What Theory Preaches

Theory has escaped academia and been unleashed upon the wider culture. But how can such obscure ideas about knowledge, power, and language survive outside the unique climate of academia and affect everyday life? Is the supermarket cashier really reading Gayatri Spivak on his lunch break? Is your doctor devouring queer Theory on the train? How likely is it that your computer technician reads feminist epistemology in his spare time or that your favorite sports commentator is well versed in critical race Theory?

Not very. Most people never engage with Theory directly, but no one is entirely safe from its influence anymore. In the United Kingdom recently, a disabled grandfather and bag packer named Brian Leach was sacked by his employer, the supermarket chain Asda, for sharing a Billy Connolly comedy skit on Facebook, which one of his colleagues felt was Islamophobic—an idea that stems from post-colonial Theory. In the United States, software engineer James Damore was fired by Google for writing an internal memo about how men and women differ psychologically on average—as an attempt to find solutions for the four-to-one gender disparity in tech. This follows from queer Theory and intersectional feminism. Meanwhile, there's a media frenzy about identity and representation in Hollywood every other day, while doctors across the Western world face the challenge of advising obese patients on their health without fat shaming them.

Examples like this crop up all the time, but many people still don't believe there's anything to worry about. They will point out that Mr. Leach was rehired, argue that Mr. Damore's views could enforce stereotypes, agree that there are representation issues in Hollywood, and say that doctors really should be more sensitive. Yes, they'll say, we hear a lot of stories about campus protests, but college students have always protested— it's practically a rite of passage. It's mostly just a few activists at elite universities who demand trigger warnings, safe spaces, and the deplatforming of everyone who disagrees with them.

Given the rise of demagoguery, populism, nationalism, and anti-intellectual currents in the mainstream right-wing and the growth of far-right movements all over Europe and beyond, should we really be worrying about a few people getting overzealous in their support of equality? Far-right terrorism is on the rise, and the alt-right and incels are proliferating online and committing serious acts of violence in real life. Shouldn't liberal lefties focus their attention there?

Yes, but refusing to admit that there are problems on the left won't help anyone. What's happening in universities is a genuine problem. These ideas are impacting the real world. Fixing the problem in the universities isn't a distraction from fighting the populist, anti-intellectual right but a vital part of it.

What Is Happening in Our Universities, and Why Does It Matter?

Critical Social Justice scholarship gets passed down to students, who take it out into the world. This effect is strongest within Critical Social Justice fields of study (whose graduates disproportionately go on to work in human resources, education, and media), but Critical Social Justice also materializes in campus culture at large. Most universities in the United States now teach these ideas to everyone as part of the general curriculum. Indeed, Critical Social Justice ideas should all sound quite familiar to any current or recent student.

We often encounter the argument that, once they get into the "real world," students will have to leave these ideological positions behind in order to find employment. But what if, instead, they act on the instruction they've received and take their ideological beliefs out into the professional world and try to remake that world accordingly? Isn't that more likely?

The real world *is* changing to absorb the skills of such students. There's already a Critical Social Justice industry worth billions of dollars dedicated to training companies and institutions to enact and police Critical Social Justice. "Diversity, Equity, and Inclusion Officers" are working in higher education, human resource departments, large private-sector companies, trade unions, municipalities, state and federal governments, and the civil service. These officers now wield significant institutional, social, and cultural power.

According to a 2017 report by the Foundation for Individual Rights in Education, more than two hundred U.S. colleges and universities publicized having "bias response teams" tasked with responding to reports of identity-based bias. These teams can only provide "education and persuasion," not punishment, but they can *indirectly* lead to sanctioning or firing by submitting bias reports to administrators with recommendations for action.

But what counts as "bias"? Students have complained about everything from other students supporting former President Donald Trump to expressions of antiracism such as "I don't see color." Because bias is operationally defined as a "state of mind," sensitivity detectors might be set a tad high. Students who have been reported generally aren't required to submit themselves for special anti-bias education, but many of them likely do to avoid backlash. They will also likely censor themselves in the future. This is terrible for fostering the healthy debate and viewpoint diversity that are essential at universities.

There have also been attempts to silence certain views on campus. "No-platforming" policies for particular political groups and certain public figures have become common. Certain political and religious views—even some academic views shared by professionals—are considered too dangerous or even "violent" to be allowed a platform.

This problem even expands to scholarship. Rebecca Tuvel wrote a paper for the feminist philosophy journal *Hypatia* that explored parallels between transgender and transracial (identifying as another race) identities. However, for Theory, race and gender are profoundly different. Being trans, according to queer Theory, means breaking down the oppressive categories of sex and gender, but claiming to be transracial is making an illegitimate claim to a lived experience of oppression. This is seen as speaking over and erasing people of color. Tuvel—an untenured assistant professor—paid the price for this misstep. Her paper was retracted and she was subjected to a vicious witch hunt. *Hypatia* suffered catastrophically for accepting the paper, too.

Bruce Gilley's case was even more extreme. After years researching postcolonial societies, mostly drawing upon scholars in genuine postcolonial locales, he wrote "The Case for Colonialism"—a nuanced paper that counterbalanced the central idea of postcolonial Theory, that colonialism is purely bad for the colonized. His paper was reviewed and accepted for publication in the scholarly journal *Third World Quarterly*. Immediately, accusations were filed against him at Portland State University, where he works, and calls were made for the paper to be unpublished, for him to lose his job, and even for his doctorate to be revoked. After receiving death threats, the journal retracted the paper.

There is good scholarship being done on gender, race, and sexuality, but Critical Social Justice ideology and activism undermines it. Some scholars say that anyone who criticizes Critical Social Justice scholarship just hates minority groups or women. Try to imagine a parallel in other fields. Do people say, "Yes, some bad papers get added to the body of medical knowledge, but there are good ones too!" instead of trying to weed out the bad papers so that people don't receive dangerous or ineffective treatments? No, because we recognize that safe and effective medicine is essential to human thriving. So is rigorous scholarship on social justice issues. Scholars in those fields should know this better than anyone.

Critical Social Justice has also affected other fields, from literature, philosophy, and history to science, technology, and engineering. Arguments have even been made that mathematics is intrinsically sexist and racist because of its focus on objectivity and proof and because of disparate outcomes in mathematics education across racial groups. One 2018 paper asserts,

> Drawing upon Indigenous worldviews to reconceptualize what mathematics is and how it is practiced, I argue for a movement against objects, truths, and knowledge towards a way of being in the world that is guided by first principles— mathematx. This shift from thinking of mathematics as a noun to mathematx as a verb holds potential for honouring our connections with each other as human and other-than-human persons, for balancing problem solving with joy, and for maintaining critical bifocality at the local and global level.

How this would improve mathematics, we have no idea, but the political agenda here is obvious and alarming. Earlier in this book, we referenced a Critical Social Justice paper that characterizes its own subject as being ideally thought of like a virus that infects other fields. Readers should know that this is how Critical Social Justice views itself. This explicit intention mirrors a doctrine named "the long march through the institutions" by German Marxist activist Rudi Dutschke in the late 1960s, who saw how a revolutionary model based on prolonged struggle that had first been proposed by Albanian-Italian Communist Antonio Gramsci in the 1920s was successfully applied by Chinese Communist dictator Mao Zedong in the Chinese Cultural Revolution (during which millions died as a result). The goal is to take over the institutions of liberal societies from within and change them into "Critical" institutions. This "long march" has already been very successful throughout the West and now threatens liberalism at its core.

Social Justice Institutionalized—A Case Study

One of the most extreme examples of Critical Social Justice activism and Theory playing out in a real-world institution is the case of Evergreen State College in Olympia, Washington. The parallels to the Chinese Cultural Revolution, in which students called the Red Guard attacked and shamed their parents, grandparents, and teachers in an effort to radically remake the culture on the spot, are undeniable. Evergreen is considered one of the most liberal universities in the United States. When biology professor Bret Weinstein objected to white people being asked to leave campus for a day in May 2017, a group of student-activists reacted angrily.

The result was mayhem: student-activists began to protest and riot all over campus. Classes were disrupted and graduation had to be held off campus. The problem escalated to the point where student-activists were barricading doors against the police, holding faculty members as de facto hostages, and stopping cars to search for Weinstein, while armed with baseball bats. Meanwhile, they claimed that "black and brown bodies" weren't safe on campus, even as the university president told the campus police to stand down and let everything happen without intervention.

The campus descended into mob madness. Most chillingly and most tellingly, protesters were both unwilling to listen to and seemingly unable to comprehend the views they were protesting against. When Weinstein asked for evidence that the campus was racist, they shouted over him and told him that the request for evidence was itself racist. Their evidence was that they lived the experience every day. Instead of making any case for their claims, the student-activists chanted Critical Social Justice slogans like "white silence is violence" and demanded that the science department be monitored, and its faculty brought in, retrained, and sanctioned for their inherently problematic views. When some students of color expressed support for Weinstein and made statements similar to his, the mob shouted them down and dismissed their lived experience because it didn't align with the "authentic" experience detailed by Theory.

There is a one-word answer to how this could have happened: Theory. The Evergreen establishment had accepted so many of the "antiracism" views of critical race educators like Robin DiAngelo—such as the idea of white fragility—that it lost its ability to defend itself against the protesters. Once enough people accused the college of being a racist institution overrun by white supremacy, the faculty and administrators had no recourse but to accept the accusation and start making the changes demanded.

What else could they do? They accepted that "the question is not 'did racism take place?' but rather 'how did racism manifest in that situation?'" so the only possible conclusion was that they were working for an intrinsically racist organization. More than four years later, Evergreen's enrollment and its reputation still haven't recovered. Just like happened with so many things in the Chinese Cultural Revolution, the institution in question was largely ruined.

How This Affects the Broader World

Unlike Vegas, what happens in the university doesn't stay in the university.

Critical Social Justice activism has gained a lot of influence over many areas of society, especially through social media. Although most people don't subscribe to Critical Social Justice ideas, these ideas are clearly influential, as demonstrated by the fact that tech, broadcasting, and retail giants will routinely buckle under pressure from Critical Social Justice advocates.

In 2019, Macy's found itself at the center of an outcry that began with just one offended person on Twitter. The retailer had to publicly apologize for producing a plate that showed portion sizes in terms of jeans sizes (which was considered "fat shaming"). They cancelled the line of products, at high cost. The Japanese noodle giant Nissin apologized for and withdrew anime that depicted a Haitian-Japanese tennis player with pale skin and European features. Gucci apologized and withdrew a sweater that some people believed looked like blackface. The same accusation was levelled at some shoes produced by singer Katy Perry, now withdrawn.

It's not surprising that large corporations have caved in so easily to Critical Social Justice pressure. Their goal is to make money, not to uphold liberal values. Since the majority of consumers in Western countries support the general idea of social justice, and since most people don't know the difference between social justice and Critical Social Justice, large corporations often decide that it's best to give in to the demands of Critical Social Justice activists. Also, just as under the Chinese Cultural Revolution, the shaming sessions, which were called "struggle sessions" in China, are terrifyingly effective when people and institutions are not ready for them.

Critical Social Justice activists are very visible on social media and keen to punish people who are influential in media and the arts. Calls for the punishment of celebrities, artists, athletes, and other prominent individuals who have transgressed against Critical Social Justice, often unknowingly, are often referred to as "cancel culture." This chilling practice often involves the utter destruction of someone's career and reputation for something she might have said decades ago, or as a teenager.

Here are some examples of celebrity "cancellations" in recent years:

- Actor Kevin Hart was forced to step down as host of the Oscars when old tweets containing gay slurs were discovered. When he was later injured in a car accident, many Critical Social Justice activists *celebrated* it.

- The lesbian TV show host Ellen DeGeneres was also targeted after she accepted Hart's apology on behalf of the LGBT community.

- Hollywood A-lister Matt Damon incurred online feminist wrath by saying that sexual assault occurred on a spectrum and that a pat on the butt was different from rape.

- Lesbian tennis superstar Martina Navratilova was attacked for arguing that it is not fair for trans women tennis players to compete against cis women.

- J. K. Rowling was condemned as a transphobe by much of social media and several of the main actors of the *Harry Potter* films for saying women's biological reality defines their experience.

- Actress and former MMA fighter Gina Carano was fired from the popular Disney series *The Mandalorian* after making a number of controversial social media posts that led the hashtag #FireGinaCarano to trend.

All of this comes from activists who have adopted Theory. The activist's job is to scrutinize texts, events, culture, activities, places, spaces, attitudes, mind-sets, phrasing, dress, and every other conceivable cultural artifact for hidden bigotry, then expose it and purge it from society.

The Critical Social Justice policing of language and thought also affects art itself. Critical Social Justice activists will calculate the proportion of women, people of color, LGBT people, disabled people, or fat people in a book or film and object if any group is underrepresented, in its view. The absence, misrepresentation, or underrepresentation of such groups is described as "erasing" minorities and "denying their validity" and as "upholding" white supremacy, patriarchy, heteronormativity, cisnormativity, ableism, or fatphobia.

But the opposite issue—*appropriation*—is also a problem. This draws on the idea of standpoint theory, in which knowledge is rooted in "lived experience." It's considered bad for artists to create or portray characters with a marginalized identity that's not their own. We often see demands that actors play characters only from their own identity groups—a straight cis woman shouldn't be allowed to play a lesbian or trans woman in a film, and an able-bodied person shouldn't play a disabled person. Critical Social Justice activists say those roles should be reserved for marginalized actors—even though acting is all about putting yourself in someone else's shoes.

Sometimes the demands made by activists are impossible to meet: J. K. Rowling was condemned for not including people of color among her main protagonists in the *Harry Potter* books, but she was also criticized for including Native American wizarding lore in them. Musicians and artists are particularly vulnerable to accusations of cultural appropriation. Madonna has been criticized for appropriating Indian and Hispanic culture and Gwen Stefani for appropriating Japanese and Native American aesthetics. Black artists aren't immune to this either. Rihanna has been accused of appropriating Chinese culture and Beyoncé of appropriating Indian Bollywood styles.

Media and art can also be negatively impacted when books, art, films, or video games are scrutinized as "discourse" and problematized on the grounds of the power dynamics they support. Of course, there really are negative stereotypes and portrayals in art, and they should be analyzed and criticized. However, much recent analysis is highly biased and too fluid. The depictions of black people in film are frequently picked apart to the point where it seems nothing is good enough. Black women being portrayed as strong or tough is seen as a negative stereotype, but black women being portrayed as weak or submissive wouldn't go down well either. Similarly, feminist scholars and activists often critique the oversexualized portrayal of women in film—while at the same time they critique certain female characters for being portrayed as "sexless"! They also uncover sexism by counting up the number of words spoken by women in comparison to men in certain films, or the amount of time women in a movie spend speaking about men.

This type of postmodern feminist analysis not only casts doubt on more rigorous and measured analyses, but can also limit the range of possible characters in film and art, including female ones. 20th Century Fox apologized for a billboard showing the *X-Men* supervillain Mystique being choked by Apocalypse after feminists complained about the "casual violence against women" portrayed in the image. A female superhero or villain would either have to not get into fights against men or win those fights without ever getting hit to meet that impossibly high standard. Similarly, the HBO show *Game of Thrones* has been criticized for Sansa Stark's experience of rape and abuse making her character stronger. Some feminists felt that this played into rape culture by somehow justifying rape. How can female characters be depicted as powerful and resilient if they are not allowed to overcome abuse, violence, and adversity?

More concerning, though, is the effect Critical Social Justice scholarship is having on disabled people. For example, a new form of autism activism is rooted in the premise that people on the autistic spectrum shouldn't be considered disabled. There is something to this argument, since many high-functioning autistic individuals have pointed out that they are perfectly valid, happy human beings who are just wired differently. However, other autistic people and their carers have pointed out that autism can often be profoundly disabling and distressing, and this new type of activism makes it harder for those more severely affected to receive support.

Others have pointed out that complicated Critical Social Justice rules about language, bias, and social interactions are often particularly difficult for autistic people to follow and that the neurologically atypical are particularly vulnerable to breaking such confusing rules. James Damore, the autistic Google engineer who responded very literally to a request for feedback on how to get more women into tech and was subsequently fired, is a good example.

Deaf activists point out that cochlear implants—which are surgically inserted into the ear canal—don't always work perfectly and can be disorienting and stressful to use, so deaf people shouldn't be pressured to tolerate them. This is fine, but some deaf activists have claimed that giving deaf kids cochlear implants is akin to genocide of deaf people and look down on deaf people who want to improve their hearing.

Mental health activists also frequently see mental illness as a marginalized identity. One problem with this approach is that people tend to get attached to their identities as mentally ill people. This may discourage some from seeking treatment and trying to recover. While activists have done good work in addressing some of the stigma attached to mental health problems, turning mental illness into an intrinsic aspect of someone's identity could be damaging.

Fat activism has a similar problem that is potentially even more dangerous. Central to fat activism is the belief that obesity is only considered unhealthy because of fat hatred and because we put too much trust in scientific discourses. This view is attractive to many dangerously obese people, particularly women, who have found it very difficult to lose weight. Rather than seek medical or psychological support, they can learn to love their bodies as they are. The body positivity movement promotes morbidly obese models as beautiful and healthy, despite the evidence of obesity's link to diabetes, heart disease, polycystic ovaries, joint and respiratory problems, and several forms of cancer. There are dozens of websites informing morbidly obese people how to find a doctor who won't tell them their weight is unhealthy.

This attitude can kill.

Cultures of Coddling and Victimhood

These examples show the postmodern principles and themes in action. Two important books, both published in 2018, address the causes, manifestations, and potential dangers of these social changes. They are *The Coddling of the American Mind: How Good Intentions and Bad Ideas Are Setting Up a Generation for Failure*, by Greg Lukianoff and Jonathan Haidt, and *The Rise of Victimhood Culture: Microaggressions, Safe Spaces, and the New Culture Wars*, by Bradley Campbell and Jason Manning. Lukianoff and Haidt focus on psychology and Campbell and Manning on sociology, so their approaches capture different aspects of the same phenomenon.

In *The Coddling of the American Mind*, Lukianoff and Haidt write about the dramatic decrease in young people's resilience and ability to cope with difficult ideas and hurt feelings. The authors say that these struggles are a painful consequence of the acceptance of three "Great Untruths":

- The belief that people are fragile ("Anything that doesn't kill you makes you weaker").

- The belief in emotional reasoning ("Always trust your feelings").

- The belief in Us versus Them ("Life is a battle between good people and evil people").

Their central thesis is that these untruths combine to produce a psychological effect that is basically the reverse of cognitive behavioral therapy (CBT). CBT helps people stop interpreting every bad thing that happens to them as a world-ending catastrophe and encourages them to put things into perspective, think about events calmly and charitably, and act appropriately. The Great Untruths, on the other hand, encourage a negative, paranoid, and self-sabotaging mind-set—which Theory can then claim is being imposed by systemic power instead of by the failures of their own bad ideas.

These, we would argue, are some of the psychological problems that arise from Theory. The belief that people are fragile and that they are weakened by unpleasant or upsetting experiences is Theorized within Critical Social Justice scholarship and activism as marginalized groups being harmed, erased, invalidated, or subjected to violence by dominant discourses. The commitment to always trusting one's feelings, rather than trying to be objective or charitable, reflects the Critical Social Justice focus on experiential over objective knowledge. Marginalized people's experiences and emotions are, for Theory, authoritative (except for when they don't support Theory). White people's experiences, emotions, and arguments—unless they agree with Critical Social Justice tenets—are considered to be signs of fragility, rather than as ethically and/or factually defensible positions. This is all underpinned by the belief that life is a battle between good people and bad people, as represented by dominant and marginalized discourses, in which some people try to maintain oppressive systems of power and privilege at the expense of others.

In *The Rise of Victimhood Culture*, Campbell and Manning

describe the different modes of social conflict resolution in different times and cultures. They look at how people relate to each other, moralize those relationships, establish their place in the world, and seek status and justice. They identify the recent emergence of a culture of victimhood, which differs from both *dignity culture* and *honor culture*.

In an honor culture, they explain, it's important not to let anyone dominate you. Thus, people are highly sensitive to slights and respond to any indication of disrespect with immediate aggression, or even violence. This kind of culture dominated the Western world for hundreds of years and is still prevalent in some non-Western cultures and in certain subcultures in the West, such as street gangs.

Afterward came dignity culture. In a dignity culture, people are encouraged to ignore most slights, be less sensitive to verbal insults, work most problems out between individuals, and resolve serious conflicts by legal means, rather than by taking matters into their own hands. Resilience is highly prized.

The new victimhood culture that Campbell and Manning see shares honor culture's sensitivity to slight but responds with a show of weakness rather than strength. It maintains dignity culture's reliance on authorities to resolve conflict, rather than taking matters into one's own hands, but it doesn't encourage ignoring slights or seeking a peaceful resolution first. In victimhood culture, status comes from being seen as victimized. This generates support and sympathy from third parties by exploiting what Campbell and Manning refer to as "the natural moral currency of victimhood." You see this in action any time you open any social media app.

In many ways, this culture of victimhood and coddling is a sign that activism for social justice (in the real sense) has become a victim of its own success. A society that worries about microaggressions and pronouns is one in which most big problems have already been solved. As Lukianoff and Haidt mention in their discussion of "safetyism," we've eradicated fatal diseases like diphtheria and polio, eliminated the use of dangerous materials like lead, and, as a result, have drastically reduced child mortality. Now parents worry about smaller things. These can still be potentially harmful, but the focus has shifted from physical harm to psychological discomfort, creating an expectation of *emotional safety*.

Similarly, we don't think it's a coincidence that the applied postmodern turn began in the late 1980s, after the Civil Rights Movement, liberal feminism, and Gay Pride had made such great progress toward racial, gender, and LGBT equality on a legal and political level. With Jim Crow laws dismantled, empire fallen, homosexuality legalized, and discrimination on the grounds of race and sex criminalized, Western society of course wanted to continue making improvements. Since the most significant legal battles had been won, however, all that remained to tackle were sexist, racist, and homophobic attitudes and discourses. Postmodernism, with its focus on discourses of power and socially constructed knowledge, was the perfect tool to address these.

As racism, sexism, and homophobia have continued to decline, deeper and deeper readings of situations and texts are needed to detect bigotry, and even more complicated Theoretical arguments are needed to combat it. This is a direct reflection of just how little social injustice actually remains.

Theory Always Looks Good on Paper

The ideas of Critical Social Justice scholarship often look good on paper. That's almost always the way with bad theories.

Take communism, for example. Communism presents the idea that an advanced and technological society can organize itself around cooperation and shared resources and minimize exploitation. The inequalities between capitalism's winners and losers can be eliminated. We can redistribute goods and services in much fairer ways, and surely the benefits will inspire all good people to participate in such a system. We just have to get everyone on script. We just all have to cooperate.

That's the theory. But, in practice, communism has generated some of the greatest atrocities of history and been responsible for the deaths of tens, if not hundreds, of millions.

Communism is a great example of the ways social theories can fail catastrophically when put into practice, even if they aspire to "the greater good." Critical Social Justice scholarship and activism are no different. On paper, they seem to say good things: let's get to the bottom of bigotry, oppression, marginalization, and injustice, and heal the world. If we could all just care a little more, and care in the right way, we could make our way to the right side of history. We just have to get everyone on script. We just have to get everyone to cooperate. We just have to ignore any problems and swear solidarity to the cause.

It isn't going to work. Critical Social Justice can't succeed because it's an overly idealistic metanarrative, but it sounds convincing enough to significantly influence society and the way it thinks about knowledge, power, and language. Why won't it work? Partly because we humans aren't as smart as we think we are, partly because most of us are idealists on at least some level, and partly because we tend to lie to ourselves when we want something to work. But Theory is a metanarrative and metanarratives are, in fact, unreliable.

The original postmodernists got that right. What they got disastrously wrong is mistaking effective and adaptive systems for metanarratives. Liberalism and science are *not* metanarratives. Liberalism and science are systems—not just neat little theories—because they're *self-skeptical* instead of *self-certain*. This is *reasoned*, not *radical*, skepticism.

Liberal systems like regulated capitalism, republican democracy, and science resolve conflicts by subjecting human economies, societies, and knowledge production to evolutionary processes that—over time, and with persistent effort—produce reliable societies, governments, and provisionally true statements about the world. The proof is that almost everything has changed for the better over the last five hundred years, especially in the West. As Theory points out, that progress has sometimes been problematic, but, as Theory doubts, it has still been *progress*.

Things are better than they were five hundred years ago, for most people most of the time, and this is undeniable.

10 LIBERALISM AS AN ALTERNATIVE TO CRITICAL SOCIAL JUSTICE
Encouraging Discussion and Debate

Postmodern Theory and liberalism don't exist alongside each other. In fact, they are almost directly at odds.

Unlike postmodern Theory, liberalism sees knowledge as something we can learn about reality, more or less objectively. It embraces accurate categorization and clarity. It values the individual and universal human values. Although left-leaning liberals tend to favor the underdog, liberalism across the board centers human dignity over victimhood. Liberalism encourages disagreement and debate and accepts the *correspondence theory of truth*—that a statement is true if it accurately describes reality. Liberalism accepts criticism, even of itself, and makes changes based on that criticism. Liberalism acts like an evolutionary process, letting the best ideas survive and the worst fade away.

Liberalism contains both features and flaws that allowed postmodern Theory to undermine it. By tolerating differences of opinion and viewpoint diversity, liberalism allows for people not to support liberalism. By insisting on freedom of debate, liberalism explicitly permits and even welcomes criticism of its own tenets. By proclaiming universal human values and the legal and political equality of all citizens, liberalism shines a light on the ways it has failed to live up to its own values and allowed some citizens to acquire vastly more political influence than others. Liberalism's openness allows for liberalism itself to be threatened, but it's the antidote to Theory.

Liberalism isn't perfect. It aims to be fair, but it can create inequities as a by-product. Capitalism, for example, is a purely liberal economic system, but when left unregulated it's a disaster. To be generous to Karl Marx, this was what he was reacting against and falsely hoped communism would overcome. The ancient Greeks also recognized that the liberal political order, democracy, is utterly tyrannical when it's not properly managed. The American system, in particular, implemented a version called *representative democracy*—a republic in which representatives are democratically elected and involving divisions of power and limitations on the powers of government. This helps prevent the system from descending into mob rule and the tyranny of the majority. These systems depend utterly on the liberal approaches to knowledge production and conflict resolution.

Liberalism is a system of conflict resolution, not a solution to human conflicts. It isn't revolutionary, but neither does it want the world to stop advancing. Instead, liberalism is always a work in progress. As it solves each problem, it moves on to new problems, continually finding new conflicts to resolve, and new goals to achieve. In this way, liberalism is kind of an evolutionary process, and processes of this kind are, by definition, always in progress and never complete. It inevitably makes mistakes, but it allows the criticism needed to correct itself. When done right, these critiques can be useful in highlighting problems before they get out of control, but critical methods like postmodern Theory exploit liberalism's openness in order to undermine it.

Many philosophers' work has helped build liberalism up to what it is today: Mary Wollstonecraft, John Stuart Mill, John Locke, Thomas Jefferson, Francis Bacon, Thomas Paine, and many, many others. They drew inspiration from earlier thinkers in other traditions, reaching all the way back to Classical Greece more than two thousand years ago, and provided concepts and arguments that continue to persuade and inspire liberals to this day. But they didn't invent liberalism, which doesn't belong to any historical period or geographical location.

The impulse toward liberalism can be found in every time and place, whenever people want to keep the good bits of a system and toss out the failures—especially when those failures constrain, oppress, or hurt people. Unfortunately, cynical Theorists can use liberalism's failures and harms as an excuse to throw out liberalism altogether.

Why Freedom of Debate Is So Important

We're used to thinking of freedom of speech as a universal human right. We naturally tend to focus on the right of the *speaker* to say what she believes without censorship or punishment, but this focus leads us sometimes to forget the importance of freedom of speech for the *listeners* or *potential listeners*—even those who *disagree* with the speaker.

This important aspect of the freedom of debate was emphasized by philosopher and political economist John Stuart Mill in his 1859 essay *On Liberty*. Mill says there are two ways censorship harms the opponents of the view being censored. First, if the opinion is correct, "they are deprived of the opportunity of exchanging error for truth." And second, if the opinion is wrong, they lose "the clearer perception and livelier impression of truth, produced by its collision with error."

Mill's first harm is simple. The second is more subtle, but very important. He illustrates it with a fascinating example.

Isaac Newton founded modern physics in 1687, writing the equations of what came to be called Newtonian mechanics, which are now taught in every freshman physics class. Over the next century, scientists collected overwhelming evidence, from both terrestrial and astronomical observations, that Newtonian physics was correct. In 1846, it was even used to predict the existence and precise location of the planet Neptune.

Suppose that, at some point in this time, the government (or even just the universities) had decided that, since Newtonian mechanics seemed to be so accurate, it would be illegal to disagree with it. In that case, Mill says, we would actually have less reason to believe in the correctness of Newtonian mechanics! The fact that Newtonian mechanics has held up in the face of free and open debate is what gives us such confidence in it:

> If even the Newtonian philosophy were not permitted to be questioned, mankind could not feel as complete assurance of its truth as they now do. The beliefs which we have most warrant for, have no safeguard to rest on, but a standing invitation to the whole world to prove them unfounded. If the challenge is not accepted, or is accepted and the attempt fails, we are far enough from certainty still; but we have done the best that the existing state of human reason admits of; we have neglected nothing that could give the truth a chance of reaching us.

But this story has an interesting twist, which Mill had no way of knowing—it turns out that Newtonian mechanics is not correct! It's an amazingly good approximation for nearly all practical purposes, but it's not exactly correct. This was discovered by Albert Einstein in 1905–1915, more than thirty years after Mill's death. Newtonian mechanics was replaced by Einstein's special and general relativity. This important advance in science might never have happened if criticism of Newton's theory had been forbidden, and we wouldn't have all the things Einstein's theories helped us invent—from radiotherapy for cancer to GPS.

Freedom of debate could be very useful for Theorists. Even if Theory is 99 percent correct and its critics 99 percent wrong, freedom of debate could help them to improve their Theory further and give them—and us—more *rational confidence* in the correctness of Theory, if it could successfully stand against opposing ideas.

Sadly, Theorists seem to just want the warm, fuzzy feeling of being right. They tend to view attempts by others to engage them in debate as *fragility* or *willful ignorance* or *privilege preserving epistemic pushback*.

Theory Doesn't Understand Liberalism

Liberalism's success comes down to a few key points: it's goal-oriented, problem-solving, self-correcting, and—despite what postmodernists think—genuinely *progressive*. While some on the far right want to halt progress (or think it's gone too far already) and some on the far left consider progress a myth and insist that life in liberal democracies is still as oppressive as it ever has been (thanks, Foucault), liberalism both appreciates progress and is optimistic that it will continue.

Liberalism might be hard to define, but illiberalism is easily recognizable in totalitarian, hierarchical, censorious, feudal, patriarchal, colonial, or theocratic states and in people who want to bring about such states, limit freedoms, or justify inequalities. Liberals oppose all of these regimes. Liberalism accepts that it will always be fighting unjust and oppressive powers and mediating between different ideas. Liberalism respects people both as individuals and as members of the human race. It values the individual and the universal, the human and humanity.

Liberalism is the marketplace of ideas, in which better ideas eventually win out, allowing society to advance. This differs from the conservative position—that some ideas are sacred (literally or otherwise) and must not be challenged—and against the postmodern position—that some ideas are dangerous and must not be spoken. Liberalism is optimistic. If we're able to get all our ideas together, with no holds barred, and encourage free expression and civil debate, we can make the world better.

The last five hundred years have showed that liberalism works. Journalist and essayist Adam Gopnik writes, "What liberalism has in its favor are the facts. Liberals get nothing accomplished—except everything, eventually." It's hard to disagree with him, with all the evidence we have that liberal methods work. Liberalism, rationalism, and empiricism, together under the banner of the "Enlightenment," have decreased human suffering through technological improvements, effective infrastructure, and medical and other scientific advances, as well as by upholding human rights.

Despite the postmodern claim that Enlightenment thinking is too confident that it has all the answers, it is, in fact, characterized by doubt and humility about humanity's capabilities. For cognitive psychologist Steven Pinker,

> It begins with skepticism. The history of human folly, and our own susceptibility to illusions and fallacies, tell us that men and women are fallible. One therefore ought to seek good reasons for believing something. Faith, revelation, tradition, dogma, authority, the ecstatic glow of subjective certainty—all are recipes for error, and should be dismissed as sources of knowledge.

Does this sound like skepticism toward metanarratives? That's because it is. Postmodernism didn't invent skepticism: it perverted it.

Some postmodernists argue that supporting the Enlightenment implies support for atrocities like slavery, genocide, and colonialism, which accompanied our "progress." This might be a good argument if it weren't for the fact that slavery, invasions, and brutal occupations have happened throughout history, and the overwhelming message of the modern period is that those things were wrong. Another common argument is that progress is a myth because Nazism, the Holocaust, and genocidal Communism all happened less than a century ago—*after* the Enlightenment. This would be reasonable if liberals were making the argument that everything that came after the Enlightenment was liberal. These atrocities actually show what happens when totalitarianism is allowed to dominate over liberalism.

Liberalism hasn't always been victorious, and it won't always prevail, but life is much better when it does. Liberalism, despite its shortcomings, is simply better for humans. It's astonishing that over the same twenty-year period (1960–1980) during which women gained access to contraception and equal pay for equal work, homosexuality was decriminalized, and racial and sexual discrimination in employment and other areas became illegal, the postmodernists emerged and declared that it was time to stop believing in liberalism, science, reason, and the myth of progress.

Let's not follow in their footsteps. Don't stop believing in liberalism, science, reason, and progress. Instead, make a real effort to defend evidence-based knowledge, reason, and consistent ethical principles.

The Principles and Themes in Light of Liberalism

Each of the postmodern principles and themes has a kernel of truth and points to a real issue, but postmodernism doesn't have the most effective solutions. Universal liberalism, fueled by science, is much better equipped to solve problems. The liberal project should accept the criticisms raised by the postmodern principles and themes and respond as it always does: by self-correcting, adapting, and progressing.

How, then, do we counter the postmodern principles and themes simply and confidently and show the world that liberal ideas should win out in the intellectual marketplace? We can start by acknowledging what Theory gets right, in order to reject its approach to the problems it highlights.

The Postmodern Knowledge Principle

The postmodern knowledge principle assumes that knowledge is a socially constructed cultural artifact. Knowledge is certainly part of the realm of ideas, and whether or not an idea is considered "true" in a certain culture says something about that culture. But there are better and worse ways to obtain knowledge about the world. The better methods—reason and evidence—are undeniably effective at determining ways to accurately describe and predict what's occurring out there, both physically and socially.

We need to reject the postmodern knowledge principle by seeing it for what it is—a language game—and go back to the general understanding that knowledge *can* be obtained through the processes of liberal science. We have evidence that science works, and it's certainly neither racist, sexist, nor imperialistic. Science and reason are not white, Western, masculine ideas, and it's racist and sexist to suggest that they are. Science and reason belong to everybody—in fact, that's why they are so valuable.

The postmodern knowledge principle does contain a kernel of insight. From Foucault's complaints about the misapplication of scientific claims about madness and sexuality to the critical race Theorists' insistence that the problems of minorities aren't being taken seriously, postmodernism is full of calls to be less brash and to *listen*. The postmodern knowledge principle exhorts us to do a better job of listening, considering, and investigating. However, we are under no obligation to "listen and believe" or to "shut up and listen." We can't give up scientific rigor, not even for the best of causes. That's not how problems get solved.

Lived experience shouldn't be ignored, but we need science and reason because people have bias and can't always examine their lived experience neutrally. For example, we can't determine the worth of a law by the lived experience of those it has helped or harmed. Both perspectives are valuable, but incomplete. The liberal approach would be to listen to both parties, consider their points carefully, and make arguments about what needs to be conserved and what reformed.

Listen and consider asks us to take seriously some important information that we might otherwise ignore, and then evaluate fairly and rationally the totality of the evidence and arguments; *listen and believe* encourages confirmation bias, depending on who we feel morally obliged to listen to. If we follow that rule, we'll get a lot of things wrong.

The Postmodern Political Principle

The postmodern political principle says that the social construction of knowledge is intimately tied to power. The more powerful culture creates the discourses that are granted legitimacy and determines what we consider to be truth and knowledge, in ways that maintain its dominance.

The postmodern political principle needs to go. Yes, harmful discourses can gain undue power, masquerade as legitimate knowledge, and thus damage society and harm people. We should be aware of this. The postmodern idea that people are born into certain discourses that shape their understanding has validity, but the idea that they learn to parrot these discourses from their positions within a power structure, without even realizing what they are doing, is prejudicial and absurd. The claim that, say, women of color who uphold Critical Social Justice ideas are "woke" and that all other women of color who don't accept those ideas have been brainwashed into employing discourses of power that oppress them is an arrogant and presumptuous idea—but that's what happens when you tie knowledge to identity and dismiss differences in opinion as people just being brainwashed.

As liberals, we don't have to do that. We can support the arguments of liberals from every identity group, and we can evaluate whether they match reality, without claiming that any single belief is representative of "women" or "people of color."

1. The Blurring of Boundaries

Being skeptical of rigid categories and boundaries is a good thing. They should be tested, prodded, pushed, and moved. But radical skepticism, which has no method of improving the accuracy of categories and just distrusts categories on principle, is unhelpful. It doesn't affect fundamental reality. Reason, on the other hand, can be used to reach conclusions, form hypothetical models, and test them. Science and reason can provide information that we can use to strengthen *liberal* arguments and debunk both socially conservative and post-modern ones.

Queer Theory's postmodern idea that categories are inher-ently oppressive is oversimplified and unjustified. If you want to argue that men and women don't fit neatly into boxes, and therefore shouldn't be limited by stereotypes traditionally as-signed to their sex, science and liberalism can be better used to argue your case. Cognitively and psychologically, men and women are massively overlapping populations with somewhat different distributions of average traits. This means we can pre-dict trends, but the data doesn't tell us much about specific in-dividuals, if anything.

To queer Theorists, who fear that a reliance on biology will restrict men and women to distinct roles, we say, "Look at the data." The data are pretty queer already. Science already knows that human variation exists and that nature tends to be messy.

2. The Focus on the Power of Language

Language has the power to convince and persuade, to change minds, and to change society, but we need to interact with others in order to find out what's true. Even the smartest humans reason poorly when alone or in ideologically homogenous groups, because we use reason mostly to justify our own beliefs, desires, and underlying intuitions. We are at our best in a group of people with different intuitions and different reasoning, when no one can get away with a self-serving assertion unchallenged. This is why we advocate a marketplace of ideas, so that humans can use the power of language to bring all their ideas together and see which ones are best.

The power to designate which ideas are good and which are forbidden is always in the hands of those who hold the majority view (or who hold political power). Banning some ideas and enforcing others is not the right way to achieve social justice. Historically, censorship has been terrible for minorities of all kinds, and there's no reason to believe that Theory contains a magic ingredient that might make censorship work differently.

3. Cultural Relativism

Some cultures do things differently. In most cases, the differences don't matter much and are interesting to learn about and share. We all live in the same world. We're humans first, humans from particular cultures second. Most of what is true about us as humans is true of all of us.

That said, it's dangerous and absurd to pretend that we can't make any judgments about the practices of a culture other than our own. Social justice can only be served if we have consistent principles. Claims that only people on the inside of a culture can critique the oppression of their own group are a failure of both empathy and ethical consistency. Believing in individual freedom and universal human rights, we can support those who advocate for liberation wherever they are. We shouldn't hesitate to support the equal rights, opportunities, and freedoms for all women, all LGBT people, and all racial and religious minorities. These values don't belong to the West—they should belong to everyone.

4. The Loss of the Individual and the Universal

Humans exist on three levels all at once: as an individual, as a member of groups, and as a member of the human race as a whole. Theorists are particularly concerned with the community level, and we would be wrong to deny that they have a point. The groups people are a part of impact how they experience the world and the opportunities available to them. While liberalism is right to proceed from the assumption that individuals have inalienable rights that are endowed upon them by virtue of their belonging to the universal class of humanity, a liberal view that focuses only on the individual and on humanity as a whole could fail to see how certain groups within society are disadvantaged, perhaps by social class or by racial or sexual identity. We should pay careful attention to the treatment of groups, but not to the exclusion of all else.

Critical Social Justice approaches that focus *solely* on group identity are doomed to fail, because people are individuals and share a common human nature. There is no singular "voice of color"—or of women, or of trans, gay, disabled, or fat people. Even a relatively small random sample drawn from any of those groups will reveal widely varying individual views. Yes, groups can be subjected to oppression, but this oppression is wrong precisely because it causes the alienation of the affected individuals' inalienable rights. Obviously the individuals who experience the oppression are the most likely to be aware of it, so we need to "listen," but we also have to "consider." More specifically, we need to listen to and consider a variety of experiences and views from members of oppressed groups, not just a single one that has been labeled "authentic" because it represents the view essentialized by Theory.

The messages of Martin Luther King, Jr., liberal feminists, and Gay Pride activists of the 1960s and 1970s were strongly liberal, individual, and universal. "I have a dream that my four little children will one day live in a nation where they will not be judged by the color of their skin, but by the content of their character," said Dr. King in his most famous speech, appealing to white Americans' pride in their country as the Land of Opportunity and their sense of fairness, and sharing their hopes for the next generation. He rightly characterized the oppression of black Americans as having rights unjustly revoked instead of as being the result of "privileges" unfairly granted to others. He called upon empathy and stressed our shared humanity. Had he, like Robin DiAngelo, asked white Americans to be "a little less white, which means a little less oppressive, oblivious, defensive, ignorant, and arrogant," would his speech have had the same effect? We don't think so. Dr. King was able to resonate with the common drives in human nature that were shared by people of all identities.

Humans are capable of great empathy and of horrifying callousness and violence. We evolved this way because we needed to cooperate within our own groups and compete with others. Our empathy is sometimes limited to those we see as members of our own tribe, and we unleash our callous disregard and violence on those seen as competitors or enemies. Liberal humanism has achieved unprecedented human equality by allowing us to expand our circles of empathy. By dividing humans into marginalized identity groups and oppressors, Critical Social Justice risks fueling our worst tendencies—our tribalism and vengefulness.

The most frustrating thing about Theory is that it tends to get literally everything backward. It treats racial categories as supremely important, which inflames racism. It depicts sex, gender, and sexuality as mere social constructions, which undermines the fact that people often come to accept sexual minorities because they realize that people are who they are naturally. Theory is highly likely to spontaneously combust at some point, but it could cause a lot of human suffering and societal damage before it does. If we lose the institutions it attacks, it could be catastrophic for our society. Historically, this has tended to leave nations at the mercy of fascists and those representing the far right of politics, who pose their own tremendous threat to liberalism.

Fuel for the Identity Politics of the Extreme Right

One of the biggest problems with the identity politics of the identitarian left is that it gives breathing room to white supremacist identity politics and right-wing extremism. White supremacist identity politics have long held that white people should hold all the power in a society, and right-wing extremist positions tend to assert that certain aspects of Western culture, including many that are illiberal, should dominate the world; that men should take a dominant role in the public sphere and women a passive one in the home; and that homosexuality is a perversion and morally bad.

Liberals spearheading the Civil Rights Movement, liberal feminism, and Gay Pride overwhelmingly won the battle of ideas concerning race, gender, and sexuality in the second half of the twentieth century. They were so successful that by the end of the first decade of the twenty-first century, mainstream conservatives had largely accepted most of this hard-won social progress, too. As recently as the 2008 U.S. presidential election, even Democratic politicians were against same-sex marriage. Yet today, it is legal in all fifty states, and it's becoming increasingly difficult to find conservatives who want to repeal it.

This dramatic and rapid change in society's conception of gender roles, race relations, and sexual freedom is still very fragile and new, and it needs protection. It took liberal feminists a long time to beat back the stereotypes about women being prone to hysteria and emotional thinking, or being too sensitive to cope in the public sphere and in need of protection from difficult ideas or people. It took far too long for racial minorities to be recognized as equal, even after the most racist laws were repealed. Lesbian, gay, bisexual, and transgender people weren't immediately accepted once their sex lives were decriminalized, their gender identities legally supported, and their committed relationships recognized in marriage. Separate from the legal battles, they fought a long cultural battle to convince social conservatives they had no "agenda" to destroy the family, heterosexuality, masculinity, or femininity.

In just a few decades, it became normal for women to have careers and be seen as competent adults. More racial minorities became professors, doctors, judges, scientists, politicians, and accountants. Increasing numbers of gay and lesbian people felt comfortable speaking of their partners socially and at work and being physically affectionate in public. The acceptance of trans people is taking longer, but the situation has been improving—at least until recently.

Now, Critical Social Justice threatens to reverse much of this progress. It does so in two ways.

First, Critical Social Justice approaches reinforce negative stereotypes by the kind of Theories it develops. Much of its feminism treats women like children—suggesting that they are fragile, timid, lack agency, and need the public sphere to be softened for them. Arguments for "research justice" based on traditional and religious beliefs, emotions, and lived experiences mostly others non-white people by suggesting science and reason aren't for them. Trying to dictate what people must believe about gender and sexuality and the language they must use to express those beliefs are rapidly creating a hostile resistance to mainstream acceptance of trans people in particular.

Second, the critical approach to Critical Social Justice encourages tribalism and hostility by its aggressively divisive approach. The civil rights movements worked so well because they used a universalist approach—everybody should have equal rights—that appealed to human intuitions of fairness and empathy. Critical Social Justice uses a simplistic identity politics approach that ascribes collective blame to dominant groups—white people are racist, men are sexist, and straight people are homophobic. This explicitly goes against the liberal value of not judging people by their race, gender, or sexuality. This kind of rhetoric could provoke a countermovement of old right-wing identity politics—"race, gender, and sexuality are important, and whiteness, maleness, and straightness are the best."

If it becomes socially acceptable to speak disparagingly of "whiteness" while seeing "anti-blackness" everywhere and calling for the punishment of anyone who can be interpreted via Theory to be exhibiting it, this will be experienced as unfair by white people. If it becomes acceptable to speak hatefully about men while being hypersensitive to anything that can be interpreted via Theory to be disparaging of women, almost half of the population (as well as much of the other half who loves them) is likely to take this badly. If cisgender people, who account for 99.5 percent of the population, are accused of transphobia for simply existing, failing to use the correct terminology, allowing genitals to influence their dating preferences, or even having non–queer Theory beliefs about gender, this is likely to result in unfair antagonism against trans people.

The extreme right has grown in recent years, especially in Europe. In our opinion, we can all help to stop its growth by not giving oxygen to other movements that also believe race, gender, and sexuality are important. Instead, we should all strengthen the liberal systems and philosophy that have worked so well for us over the past fifty years. Reasonable, moderate voices from the left, center, and center-right should speak up to prevent authoritarian far-right backlash at all costs.

So … What Can We Do?

We think the answer is a liberal principle called *secularism*, broadly construed.

Secularism is usually understood merely as a legal principle: the "separation of church and state." The principle of secularism is based on a profound philosophical idea—that even if you think you're in possession of the truth, you have no right to impose your belief on society as a whole. Along with this comes the right to reject and criticize ideas. In a secular society, no one should be punished for rejecting religion or any other ideology.

Like a religion, Critical Social Justice has stopped searching for knowledge because it already believes it has The Truth. It's one thing to believe that knowledge is a cultural construct used to enforce power, and that this can be unjust—that's an idea that can be taken into the marketplace of ideas. But it's another thing to take this belief as a given and say that disagreeing is an act of dominance and oppression. It's even worse to say that disagreeing means being complicit in moral evil, or sin. Secularism means that no one should be required to accept or pay lip service to a belief they don't share.

We advocate two approaches to the problem of Critical Social Justice. First, we must oppose its belief system becoming a part of institutions like the government and the university, which is challenging because this has already mostly happened. As liberals, we must defend people's right to disbelieve in Critical Social Justice, just as we must defend the right of people to believe in it if they so choose. All public institutions and organizations should require their students, employees, and users not to discriminate against *anyone* and to uphold equality, but they should not require formal Critical Social Justice–based statements of belief in diversity, equity, and inclusion, or mandate diversity or equity training—neither should they assess whether discrimination has occurred merely by observing that differences in average outcomes by groups exist. We should oppose these formal statements of belief in the same way we would oppose required belief in Christianity, Islam, or Scientology, or mandatory church, mosque, or audit attendance, and we should oppose oversimplistic claims of discrimination that ignore the roles played by individual choices and the intentions of those involved in enacting policies.

Second, we must do fair battle with the ideas in Critical Social Justice. We don't believe that bad ideas can be defeated by being repressed. They must be faced head-on, the way a knight must face a dragon in order to defeat it. Rather than with swords, defeating Critical Social Justice is possible if we arm ourselves with reason, liberalism, equality, merit, and secularism. This includes allowing the difficult conversation about what aspects of Critical Social Justice should not receive state sponsorship by being forwarded through taxpayer money—a matter on which liberals can disagree. Only through these powerful tools can we expose the bad ideas in Critical Social Justice and perhaps, in time, rescue what is useful in Critical Social Justice scholarship and reform it.

Conclusion: Principled Responses to Social Injustice

Theory promises a revolution. Liberalism isn't as sexy—small, slow improvements can feel so inadequate when there are people suffering *right now*—but it's right.

You don't need to become an expert in all the great liberal thinkers, nor do you need to endlessly study Theory and Critical Social Justice in order to refute it. What you do need is a little knowledge and a significant amount of courage. You need to recognize Theory when you see it and take the liberal stance—which might just mean saying, "No, that's your belief, and I don't have to go along with it." Contrary to popular belief (within Critical Social Justice, anyway), this does not make you a bad person. It makes you *your own person*.

To make this easier, we'd like to close with a few examples of how you can recognize social injustice, while rejecting Critical Social Justice's solutions to it. Each example begins with a common Critical Social Justice talking point and follows with statements you can use to express your support for the fight against injustice, while taking the liberal path.

We hope this helps you fight the good fight.

Questions of Race and Racism

Theory-Based Claim: "Our society is inherently racist."

Principled Response: "Racism is still a problem in society and needs to be addressed but racism is widely regarded negatively."

Theory-Based Claim: "To fix racial issues, white people should acknowledge and dismantle their racism."

Principled Response: "Racial issues are best solved using evidence-based approaches to consistently oppose racial discrimination."

Theory-Based Claim: "Racism is 'power plus prejudice.'"

Principled Response: "Racism is 'prejudiced attitudes and discriminatory behavior against individuals or groups on the grounds of race.'"

Theory-Based Claim: "Everyone plays a part in perpetuating racism all the time."

Principled Response: "I disagree that racism exists in all interactions between all people of different races."

Theory-Based Claim: "The best way to deal with racism is to recognize everyone as a member of a racial group."

Principled Response: "The best way to deal with racism is to see one another as individuals and fellow humans and not primarily as racial categories."

Theory-Based Claim: "All white people are racist."

Principled Response: "Making negative generalizations about identity groups, even majority groups, is always bad."

Questions of Sex and Sexism

Theory-Based Claim: "The modern world is misogynistic."

Principled Response: "Sexist attitudes still exist in society and need to be opposed."

Theory-Based Claim: "There's no difference between men and women."

Principled Response: "Men and women are far more similar than they are different, but there are still some differences."

Theory-Based Claim: "Any time there's a gap between men's and women's achievements, it's a sign of sexist discrimination."

Principled Response: "Sexist discrimination can happen, but not every gap in outcomes between men and women is a sign that sexist discrimination happened."

Theory-Based Claim: "Sexist language oppresses women."

Principled Response: "Sexist language is wrong, but it isn't only used against women and can be opposed with language that opposes sexism."

Questions of LGBT Identity and Anti-LGBT Bigotry

Theory-Based Claim: "Homophobia and transphobia are everywhere."

Principled Response: "Discrimination and bigotry against sexual minorities are still a problem in society but most people recognize this as wrong."

Theory-Based Claim: "There would be less bigotry if everyone just realized gender (or even sex) is a social construct."

Principled Response: "It would be a much better world if more people were accepting of gender atypical people, but this is not best achieved by denying differences to exist between men and women on average due to biology."

Theory-Based Claim: "Being LGBT is a political statement to push back against sexual norms."

Principled Response: "Being LGBT is a naturally occurring variation and we should accept LGBT people the way they are as individuals without turning this natural variation into a political statement."

Theory-Based Claim: "If someone says they have a particular gender identity, that's their lived experience and must be accepted."

Principled Response: "While there is seldom any need to question any individual's gender identity, many scientists of sex and gender are concerned that gender dysphoria among young people is not necessarily best treated by uncritical acceptance and affirmation of a transgender identity but by more careful exploration and evaluation."

Theory-Based Claim: "Being straight and cisgender supports cisheteronormativity and is problematic."

Principled Response: "Being straight and cisgender is a naturally occurring variation (that is statistically very probable), and we should accept straight and cisgender people as they are as individuals without turning their gender identity or sexuality into a political statement."

Theory-Based Claim: "My pronouns are [whatever they are], and you have to respect them."

Principled Response: "I respect your personhood and will do you the courtesy of respecting the pronouns you say identify you so long as you respect my personhood and my right not to be compelled to hold any particular belief or make any particular statement, including of your pronouns."

Questions of Approach to Social Justice

Theory-Based Claim: "If you don't believe Critical Social Justice approaches are the way to oppose racism, sexism, and other bigotries, you're racist/sexist/bigoted."

Principled Response: "I think liberal humanism is the best way to oppose racism, sexism, and other bigotries and if you disagree with me, we could discuss our differences, making reasoned and evidenced arguments for our own positions and carefully considering each other's views."

GLOSSARY

Critical Theory: An analytical approach developed in the 1930s by neo-Marxist philosophers in the Institute for Social Research (Frankfurt School) derived from Karl Marx's "critical philosophy." Critical Theory is distinguished (by German philosopher Max Horkheimer) from "traditional theory" under another of Marx's dictates—"The philosophers have only interpreted the world, in various ways. The point, however, is to change it." (This is inscribed on Marx's tombstone.) That is, traditional theory is for *understanding the world as it is* and Critical Theory is for aiming to change it (in a particular way). For a theory to qualify as a Critical Theory, it must meet all of three criteria: (1) it must hold an idealized (utopian) vision for society; (2) it must describe how the existing society falls short of that vision and attempts to bring it into reality; and (3) it must inspire social activism consistent with bringing this vision into the world and consistent with the theory (what Marx referred to as "praxis").

Cultural/social constructivism: An approach to knowledge that assumes that what we think is true has actually been constructed by power dynamics in society and culture. This stands in opposition to the scientific view that there are objective truths that we can get closer to using evidence and reason. Example: the belief that men are only socialized to be violent and are no more naturally inclined toward violence than women, whether due to evolutionary or hormonal factors, is a cultural or social constructivist view. Taking this approach with the additional perspective and methods of Critical Theory is called *critical constructivism*, which is the academic term for what we have called "applied postmodernism" throughout this book.

Discourse: The way something is spoken about, or the greater cultural context surrounding a topic that signal how that topic is viewed. Example: scientific or Christian discourses refer to ways of speaking that use the terminology and assumptions of science or of Christianity. For the postmodernists, certain discourses gain undue power, and this maintains oppressive power structures. Think of the way discourses around homosexuality have changed from sinfulness to a medical disorder to just something some people are.

Empirical: A way of looking at things using evidence. Example: the high correlation of lung disease with smoking, discovered through study and experiments, is empirical evidence that smoking causes disease.

Epistemology: The study of knowledge and particularly the ways in which we determine what is and isn't knowledge.

Hegemony: The soft (but overwhelming) power of culture as mediated through its norms, beliefs, expectations, practices, and institutions. That is, "the way things are."

Metanarrative: Large overarching explanations for things that take the form of a cohesive story.

Normativity: The practice of designating some practices—for example, heterosexuality—as normal and thus deeming them proper, desirable, or virtuous, and enforcing them socially.

Pedagogy: The art of teaching.

Praxis: Activism in line with a particular Theoretical vision. The combination of Theory and activism.

Problematize: To find ethical problems in something and then to point the problems out to make them visible to others.

Standpoint theory: The theory that knowledge comes from someone's identity, which is assumed to be related to their social status or position in society.

Theory: In the context of this book, capitalized "Theory" refers to the body of postmodern philosophical literature.

NOTES

Introduction

12   [Rawls] thought a socially just society would be one where any-one would be equally happy to be born into any social milieu or identity group, whether at the top or bottom of the society: John Rawls, *A Theory of Justice* (Oxford: Oxford University Press, 1999).

12   "Critical Social Justice" is a term coined by two academics in education, Özlem Sensoy and Robin DiAngelo, and draws on the history of "critical consciousness," which means roughly the same as "Woke"—being able to see invisible systems of power and privilege based on identity. See Özlem Sensoy and Robin DiAngelo, *Is Everyone Really Equal? An Introduction to Key Concepts in Social Justice Education*, 2nd ed. (New York: Teachers College Press, 2017). For more, see Helen Pluckrose, "What Do We Mean by Critical Social Justice," Counterweight, February 17, 2021, counterweightsupport.com/2021/02/17/what-do-we-mean-by-critical-social-justice/.

15   "The master's tools will never dismantle the master's house": Audre Lorde, *Sister Outsider: Essays and Speeches* (Berkeley, CA: Crossing Press, 2007), 110–114.

1 Postmodernism

18 "a late 20th-century movement characterized by broad skepticism": Brian Duignan, "Postmodernism," *Encyclopedia Britannica*, July 19, 2019, britannica.com/topic/postmodernism-philosophy (accessed August 15, 2019).

22 "A broad social and cultural shift is taking place": Steven Seidman, ed., *The Postmodern Turn: New Perspectives on Social Theory* (Cambridge: Cambridge University Press, 1998), 1.

22 "We are in the midst of a great, confusing, stressful and enormously promising historical transition": Walter Truett Anderson, *The Fontana Postmodernism Reader* (London: Fontana Press, 1996), 2.

25 Works cited by Foucault: *Madness and Civilization: A History of Insanity in the Age of Reason,* trans. Richard Howard and Jean Kafka (New York: Routledge, 2001); *Birth of the Clinic: An Archaeology of Medical Perception,* trans. A. M. Sheridan Smith (London: Tavistock, 1975); *The Archaeology of Knowledge: And the Discourse on Language,* trans. A. M. Sheridan Smith (London: Tavistock, 1972).

27 "strict interlinkage": Jean-François Lyotard, *The Postmodern Condition: A Report on Knowledge* (Manchester: Manchester University Press, 1991).

29 "My point is not that everything is bad": Michel Foucault, "On the Genealogy of Ethics: An Overview of Work in Progress," afterword to *Michel Foucault: Beyond Structuralism and Hermeneutics,* 2nd ed., by Hubert L. Dreyfus and Paul Rabinow (Chicago: University of Chicago Press, 1983).

30 "Our hypothesis . . . should not be accorded": Lyotard, *Postmodern Condition,* 7.

31 "there is nothing [read: no meaning] outside of text": Jacques Derrida, *Of Grammatology,* trans. Gayatri Chakravorty Spivak (Baltimore: Johns Hopkins University Press, 1976). Brackets added.

31 "the death of the author": Roland Barthes, "The Death of the Author," *Aspen*, no. 5–6, ubu.com/aspen/aspen5and6/threeEssays. html.

2 Postmodernism's Applied Turn

36 A branch of feminism pioneered by African American scholars: see, for example, Patricia Hill Collins, *Black Feminist Thought: Knowledge, Consciousness, and the Politics of Empowerment* (New York: Routledge, 2015).

39 "*Je pense, donc je suis*": René Descartes, *Discourse on the Method: The Original Text with English Translation* (Erebus Society, 2017).

40 Essay by Kimberlé Crenshaw: "Mapping the Margins: Intersectionality, Identity Politics, and Violence against Women of Color," *Stanford Law Review* 43, no. 6 (1991).

43 Therefore, in this view, it's a moral obligation: Andrew Jolivétte, *Research Justice: Methodologies for Social Change* (Bristol, UK: Policy Press, 2015).

43 "epistemic justice": Miranda Fricker, *Epistemic Injustice: Power and the Ethics of Knowing* (Oxford: Oxford University Press, 2007).

43 "epistemic oppression": Kristie Dotson, "Conceptualizing Epistemic Oppression," *Social Epistemology* 28, no. 2 (2014).

43 "epistemic exploitation": Nora Berenstain, "Epistemic Exploitation," *Ergo* 3, no. 22 (2016).

43 "epistemic violence": Gayatri Chakravorty Spivak, "Can the Subaltern Speak?" in *Marxism and the Interpretation of Culture*, ed. Cary Nelson and Lawrence Grossberg (Chicago: University of Illinois Press, 1988).

45 Paper cited: Breanne Fahs and Michael Karger, "Women's Studies as Virus: Institutional Feminism, Affect, and the Projection of Danger," *Multidisciplinary Journal of Gender Studies* 5, no. 1 (2016).

46 American engineers have been fired: Sean Stevens, "The Google Memo: What Does the Research Say about Gender Differences?" *Heterodox Academy*, February 2, 2019, heterodoxacademy.org/the-google-memo-what-does-the-research-say-about-gender-differences/.

46 British comedians have been sacked: Emma Powell and Patrick Graham-Green, "Danny Baker Fired by BBC Radio 5 Live over Racist Royal Baby Tweet," *Evening Standard*, May 9, 2019.

3 Postcolonial Theory

49 Works by Frantz Fanon: *Black Skin, White Masks*, trans. Richard Philcox (New York: Penguin Books, 2019); *A Dying Colonialism*, trans. Haakon Chevalier (Middlesex: Penguin Books, 1970); *The Wretched of the Earth*, trans. Constance Farrington (Harmondsworth: Penguin, 1967).

51 Book by Edward Said: *Orientalism* (London: Penguin, 2003).

51 Said drew primarily on Fanon and Foucault: Mathieu E. Courville, "Genealogies of Postcolonialism: A Slight Return from Said and Foucault Back to Fanon and Sartre," *Studies in Religion/Sciences Religieuses* 36, no. 2 (2007).

51 Joseph Conrad, *Heart of Darkness and Other Stories* (New York: Barnes & Noble, 2019).

52 "My argument is that history is made by men and women": Said, *Orientalism*, xviii.

53 "strategic essentialism": Gayatri Chakravorty Spivak, "Subaltern Studies: Deconstructing Historiography," in *Selected Subaltern Studies*, ed. Ranajit Guha and Gayatri Chakravorty Spivak (New York: Oxford University Press, 1988), 13.

53 "Derrida marks radical critique": Spivak, "Can the Subaltern Speak?" 308.

54 "If, for a while, the ruse of desire is calculable": The Bad Writing Contest, www.denisdutton.com/bad_writing.htm.

55 "Is the language of theory merely another power ploy": Homi
    K. Bhabha, *The Location of Culture* (London: Routledge, 1994),
    20–21.

55 "Nature has made a race of workers": Joseph-Ernest Renan,
    La Réforme intellectuelle et morale (1871), as quoted in Ahdaf
    Soueif, "The Function of Narrative in the War on Terror," in *War
    on Terror,* ed. Christ Miller (Manchester: Manchester University
    Press, 2009), 30.

58 It can refer to efforts to include more scholars: Mariya Hussain,
    "Why Is My Curriculum White?" National Union of Students,
    March 11, 2015; Malia Bouattia and Sorana Vieru, "#Liberate-
    MyDegree @ NUS Connect," *NUS Connect.*

59 *alternative ways of thinking:* Gurminder K. Bhambra, Dalia Ge-
    brial, and Kerem Nişancioğlu, eds., *Decolonising the University*
    (London: Pluto Press, 2018), 1–2.

60 "The neglect of Black knowledge by society": Kehinde Andrews,
    "Introduction," in *Rhodes Must Fall: The Struggle to Decolonise
    the Racist Heart of Empire,* ed. Roseanne Chantiluke, Brian Kwo-
    ba, and Athinangamso Nkopo (London: Zed Books, 2018), 4.

61 "The public's sense of what history is": Dalia Gebrial, "Rhodes
    Must Fall: Oxford and Movements for Change," in *Decolonising
    the University,* ed. Gurminder K. Bhambra, Dalia Gebrial, and
    Kerem Nişancioğlu (London: Pluto Press, 2018), 24.

64 "'[R]esearch justice'" is a strategic framework": Andrew Jolivé-
    tte, *Research Justice: Methodologies for Social Change* (Bristol,
    UK: Policy Press, 2015), 5.

65 "These works stand at the center": Kagendo Mutua and Beth
    Blue Swadener, *Decolonizing Research in Cross-Cultural Con-
    texts: Critical Personal Narratives* (Albany, NY: SUNY Press,
    2011).

65 "[F]rom the vantage point of the colonised": Ibid., 2.

67 "modern science is as much a local tradition of the West": Meera
    Nanda, "We Are All Hybrids Now: The Dangerous Epistemol-

ogy of Post-colonial Populism," *Journal of Peasant Studies* 28, no. 2 (2001): 165.

67 "Postmodern/post-colonial theory's animus": Ibid., 165.

70 They probably wouldn't have any use for an ideology: Alan J. Bishop, "Western Mathematics: The Secret Weapon of Cultural Imperialism," *Race & Class* 32, no. 2 (1990); Laura E. Donaldson, "Writing the Talking Stick: Alphabetic Literacy as Colonial Technology and Postcolonial Appropriation," *American Indian Quarterly* 22, no. 1/2 (1998); Lucille Toth, "Praising Twerk: Why Aren't We All Shaking Our Butt?" *French Cultural Studies* 28, no. 3 (2017).

4 Queer Theory

79 "*whatever* is at odds with the normal": David M. Halperin, *Saint Foucault: Towards a Gay Hagiography* (New York: Oxford University Press, 1997), 62.

79 As evolutionary biologist E. O. Wilson states: E. O. Wilson, "From Sociobiology to Sociology," in *Evolution, Literature, and Film: A Reader*, ed. Brian, Joseph Carroll, and Jonathan Gottschall (New York: Columbia University Press, 2010), 98.

81 "The society that emerged in the nineteenth century": Michel Foucault, *The History of Sexuality: Volume 1: An Introduction*, trans. Robert J. Hurley (New York: Penguin, 1990), 69.

81 Foucault called this "biopower": Ibid., 54.

81 "Power is everywhere": Ibid., 93.

82 Essay by Gayle Rubin: "Thinking Sex: Notes for a Radical Theory of the Politics of Sexuality," in *The Lesbian and Gay Studies Reader*, ed. Henry Abelove, Michèle Aina Barale, and David M. Halperin (Abingdon: Taylor & Francis, 1993).

84 Books by Judith Butler: *Bodies That Matter: On the Discursive Limits of "Sex"* (New York: Routledge, 1993); *Gender Trouble* (London: Routledge, 2006).

85   For Butler, the mission of queer Theory: Judith Butler, *Bodies That Matter*, 192–3.

85   Adrienne Rich's concept of *compulsory heterosexuality:* Adrienne Rich, *Compulsory Heterosexuality and Lesbian Existence* (Denver, CO: Antelope Publications, 1982).

85   As a solution, Butler proposed: *Gender Trouble*, 169.

87   "In consonance with my emphasis": Eve Kosofsky Sedgwick, *Epistemology of the Closet* (Berkeley, CA: University of California Press, 2008), 13.

88   "An assumption underlying the book": Ibid., 3.

91   "gender intersects with": *Gender Trouble*, 4.

5 Critical Race Theory and Intersectionality

99   Books by Derrick Bell: *Race, Racism, and American Law* (Boston: Little, Brown, and Co., 1984); *And We Are Not Saved: The Elusive Quest for Racial Justice* (New York: Basic Books, 2008).

100 They frequently advocate Black Nationalism and segregation: Mark Stern and Khuram Hussain, "On the Charter Question: Black Marxism and Black Nationalism," *Race Ethnicity and Education* 18, no. 1 (2014).

102 Book-length essay by Patricia J. Williams: *The Alchemy of Race and Rights* (Cambridge, MA: Harvard University Press, 1991).

102 Reader by Richard Delgado and Jean Stefancic: *Critical Race Theory: An Introduction*, 3rd ed. (New York: New York University Press, 2017).

106 Black feminist scholar and activist bell hooks, for example, wrote: bell hooks, "Postmodern Blackness," in *The Fontana Postmodern Reader,* ed. Walter Truett Anderson (London: Fontana Press, 1996), 117.

106 Paper by Kimberlé Crenshaw: "Demarginalizing the Intersection of Race and Sex: A Black Feminist Critique of Antidiscrimination Doctrine, Feminist Theory and Antiracist Politics," *Uni-*

versity of Chicago Legal Forum 1, no. 8 (1989), chicagounbound. uchicago.edu/uclf/vol1989/iss1/8.

107 Essay by Kimberlé Crenshaw: "Mapping the Margins: Intersectionality, Identity Politics, and Violence against Women of Color," *Standford Law Review* 43, no. 6 (1991): 1224n9.

112 Gay white men and non-black people of color are told: Adam Fitzgerald, "Opinion: Time for Cis-Gender White Men to Recognize Their Privilege," *news.trust.org*, May 2, 2019, news.trust. org/item/20190502130719-tpcky/; Jezzika Chung, "How Asian Immigrants Learn Anti-Blackness from White Culture, and How to Stop It," *Huffington Post*, September 7, 2017, www.huffpost.com/entry/how-asian-americans-can-stop-contributing-to-anti-blackness_b_599f0757e4b0cb7715bfd3d4.

112 Lighter-skinned black people are told: Kristel Tracey, "We Need to Talk about Light-skinned Privilege," *Media Diversified*, February 7, 2019, mediadiversified.org/2018/04/26/we-need-to-talk-about-light-skinned-privilege/.

112 Straight black men have been described as: Damon Young, "Straight Black Men Are the White People of Black People," *Root*, September 19, 2017, verysmartbrothas.theroot.com/straight-black-men-are-the-white-people-of-black-people-1814157214.

112 trans men ... now have male privilege: Miriam J. Abelson, "Dangerous Privilege: Trans Men, Masculinities, and Changing Perceptions of Safety," *Sociological Forum* 29, no. 3 (2014).

112 Gay men and lesbians might soon find themselves: Sara C., "When You Say 'I Would Never Date a Trans Person,' It's Transphobic. Here's Why," *Medium*, November 11, 2018, medium. com/@QSE/when-you-say-i-would-never-date-a-trans-person-its-transphobic-here-s-why-aa6fdcf59aca.

113 Asians and Jews are losing their "marginalized" status: Iris Kuo, "The 'Whitening' of Asian Americans," *Atlantic*, September 13, 2018, www.theatlantic.com/education/archive/2018/08/the-whitening-of-asian-americans/563336/; Paul Lungen, "Check Your Jewish Privilege," *Canadian Jewish News*, December 21,

2018, www.cjnews.com/living-jewish/check-your-jewish-privilege.

113 Queerness needs to be decolonized: Zachary Small, "Joseph Pierce on Why Academics Must Decolonize Queerness," *Hyperallergic*, August 10, 2019, hyperallergic.com/512789/joseph-pierce-on-why-academics-must-decolonize-queerness/.

113 Peter Tatchell criticized black rappers: Peter Tatchell, "Tag: Stop Murder Music," *Peter Tatchell Foundation,* May 13, 2016, www.petertatchellfoundation.org/tag/stop-murder-music/.

113 [E]thnic minority beauticians declined bikini wax services: Arwa Mahdawi, "It's Not a Hate Crime for a Woman to Feel Uncomfortable Waxing Male Genitalia," *Guardian,* July 27, 2019, www.theguardian.com/commentisfree/2019/jul/27/male-genitalia-week-in-patriarchy-women.

113 Book by Ange-Marie Hancock: *Intersectionality: An Intellectual History* (New York: Oxford University Press, 2016).

114 Book by Jonathan Haidt and Greg Lukianoff: *The Coddling of the American Mind: How Good Intentions and Bad Ideas Are Setting Up a Generation for Failure* (New York: Penguin Books, 2019).

115 "the question is not 'did racism take place?'": Heather Bruce, Robin DiAngelo, Gyda Swaney (Salish), and Amie Thurber, "Between Principles and Practice: Tensions in Anti-Racist Education," presentation at the 2014 Race and Pedagogy National Conference, soundideas.pugetsound.edu/race_pedagogy/23/.

6 Feminisms and Gender Studies

123 Books cited: Simone de Beauvoir, *The Second Sex*, trans. H. M. Parshley (New York: Vintage Books, 1974); Betty Friedan, *The Feminine Mystique* (New York: W. W. Norton & Company, 2013); Kate Millett, Catharine A. MacKinnon, and Rebecca Mead, *Sexual Politics* (New York: Columbia University Press, 2016); Germaine Greer, *The Female Eunuch* (London: Fourth Estate, 2012).

125 "'women' and 'men' are regarded as constructions": Jane Pilcher and Imelda Whelehan, *Key Concepts in Gender Studies* (Los Angeles: Sage, 2017), xiii.

128 Paper by Candace West and Don H. Zimmerman: "Doing Gender," *Gender and Society* 1, no. 2 (1987).

130 "When the women's movement began in the late 60s": bell hooks, "Racism and Feminism: The Issue of Accountability," in *Making Sense of Women's Lives: An Introduction to Women's Studies*, ed. Lauri Umansky, Paul K. Longmore, and Michele Plott (Lanham, MD: Rowman & Littlefield, 2000).

130 Book by Patricia Hill Collins: *Black Feminist Thought: Knowledge, Consciousness, and the Politics of Empowerment* (New York: Routledge, 2015).

131 "The longstanding effort to 'colorize' feminist theory": Patricia Hill Collins, "Toward a New Vision: Race, Class, and Gender as Categories of Analysis and Connection," *Race, Sex & Class* 1, no. 1 (1993).

132 Essay by Peggy McIntosh: "White Privilege: Unpacking the Invisible Knapsack," in *On Privilege, Fraudulence, and Teaching As Learning: Selected Essays 1981–2019* (New York: Taylor & Francis, 2019), 29–34.

133 "Some criticism is ill-informed": Linda Gordon, "'Intersectionality,' Socialist Feminism and Contemporary Activism: Musings by a Second-Wave Socialist Feminist," *Gender & History* 28, no. 2 (2016), 351.

134 Terry Kupers on masculinity in prisons: Terry A. Kupers, "Toxic Masculinity as a Barrier to Mental Health Treatment in Prison," *Journal of Clinical Psychology* 61, no. 6 (2005).

135 "inclusive masculinity": Eric Anderson, *Inclusive Masculinity: The Changing Nature of Masculinities* (London: Routledge, 2012).

7 Disability and Fat Studies

141 "[E]xperiences will undoubtedly be culturally located": Michael Oliver, Bob Sapey, and Pam Thomas, *Social Work with Disabled People* (Basingstoke: Palgrave Macmillan, 2012), 19.

143 "Like compulsory heterosexuality": Robert McRuer, *Crip Theory: Cultural Signs of Queerness and Disability* (New York: New York University Press, 2006), 8.

143 Book by Dan Goodley: *Disability Studies: Theorising Disablism and Ableism* (New York: Routledge, 2014).

145 Book by Fiona Campbell: *Contours of Ableism: The Production of Disability and Abledness.* (New York: Palgrave Macmillan, 2012).

146 Excerpt from Lydia X. Y. Brown: in Jennifer Scuro, *Addressing Ableism: Philosophical Questions via Disability Studies* (Lanham, MD: Lexington Books, 2019), 70.

147 Book by Joseph Shapiro: *No Pity: People with Disabilities Forging a New Civil Rights Movement* (New York: Times Books, 1994).

148 Excerpt from dialogue between Lydia X. Y. Brown and Jennifer Scuro: *Addressing Ableism: Philosophical Questions via Disability Studies* (Lanham, MD: Lexington Books, 2019), 70.

152 Book by Lindo Bacon: *Health at Every Size: The Surprising Truth about Your Weight* (Dallas, TX: BenBella Books, 2010).

153 Book by Charlotte Cooper: *Fat Activism: A Radical Social Movement* (Bristol, England: HammerOn Press, 2016).

153 Quote from Marilyn Wann: "Foreword," in *The Fat Studies Reader*, ed. Esther D. Rothblum and Sondra Solovay (New York: New York University Press, 2009), xi.

155 "That fat and queer people would heartily embrace": Kathleen LeBesco, "Quest for a Cause: The Fat Gene, the Gay Gene, and the New Eugenics," in *The Fat Studies Reader*, 70.

156 "have instead chosen to engage poetry": Lucy Aphramor and Jacqui Gringas, "Disappeared Feminist Discourses on Fat in Dietetic Theory and Practice," in *The Fat Studies Reader*, 97.

156 "rethink of how dietetic attitudes": Ibid., 100.

156 "Although we do not wholly reject": John Coveney and Sue Booth, *Critical Dietetics and Critical Nutrition Studies* (Cham, Switzerland: Springer, 2019), 18.

8 Critical Social Justice Scholarship and Thought

168 "focusing on propositional knowledge": Alexis Shotwell, "Forms of Knowing and Epistemic Resources," in *The Routledge Handbook of Epistemic Injustice*, ed. Ian James Kid, José Medina, and Gaile Pohlhaus, Jr. (London: Routledge, 2017), 79.

171 Book by Barbara Applebaum: *Being White, Being Good: White Complicity, White Moral Responsibility, and Social Justice Pedagogy* (Lanham, MD: Lexington Books, 2010).

174 Essay by Alison Bailey: "Tracking Privilege-Preserving Epistemic Pushback in Feminist and Critical Race Philosophy Classes," *Hypatia* 32, no. 4 (2017).

177 Essay by Robin DiAngelo: "White Fragility," *International Journal of Critical Pedagogy* 3, no. 3 (2011); book by Robin DiAngelo: *White Fragility: Why It's So Hard for White People to Talk about Racism* (London: Allen Lane, 2019).

9 Critical Social Justice in Action

184 which one of his colleagues felt was Islamophobic: Hardeep Singh, "Why Was a Disabled Grandad Sacked by Asda for Sharing a Billy Connolly Clip?" *Spectator*, June 27, 2019, blogs.spectator.co.uk/2019/06/why-was-a-disabled-grandad-sacked-by-asda-for-sharing-a-billy-connolly-clip/.

185 James Damore was fired by Google: Sean Stevens, "The Google Memo: What Does the Research Say about Gender Differences?" *Heterodox Academy*, February 2, 2019, heterodoxacademy.org/the-google-memo-what-does-the-research-say-about-gender-differences/.

185 media frenzy about identity and representation in Hollywood: Charlotte Zoller, "How I Found a Fat-Positive Doctor Who Didn't Just Tell Me to Lose Weight," *Vice*, August 15, 2018, www.vice.com/en_us/article/43ppwj/how-to-find-a-fat-positive-doctor.

185 Far-right terrorism is on the rise: Daniel Koehler, "Violence and Terrorism from the Far-Right: Policy Options to Counter an Elusive Threat," *Terrorism and Counter-Terrorism Studies* (February 2019), doi.org/10.19165/2019.2.02.

187 can only provide "education and persuasion": Ryan Miller et al., "Bias Response Teams: Fact vs. Fiction," *Inside Higher Ed*, June 17, 2019, www.insidehighered.com/views/2019/06/17/truth-about-bias-response-teams-more-complex-often-thought-opinion.

187 sensitivity detectors might be set a tad high: Jeffrey Aaron Snyder and Amna Khalid, "The Rise of 'Bias Response Teams' on Campus," *New Republic*, March 30, 2016, newrepublic.com/article/132195/rise-bias-response-teams-campus.

188 Her paper was retracted: "Hypatia Editorial Office," archive.is, June 9, 2017, archive.is/kVrLb.

188 *Hypatia* suffered catastrophically: Jerry Coyne, "Journal Hypatia's Editors Resign, and Directors Suspend Associate Editors over Their Apology for the 'Transracialism' Article," *Why Evolution Is True*, July 22, 2017, whyevolutionistrue.wordpress.com/2017/07/22/journal-hypatias-editors-resign-and-directors-suspend-associate-editors-over-their-apology-for-the-transracialism-article/.

188 calls were made for the paper to be unpublished: Kelly Oliver, "If This Is Feminism . . ." *Philosophical Salon*, May 9, 2017, thephilosophicalsalon.com/if-this-is-feminism-its-been-hijacked-by-the- thought-police/.

188 the journal retracted the paper: Peter Wood, "The Article That Made 16,000 Ideologues Go Wild," *Minding the Campus*, October 18, 2017, www.mindingthecampus.org/2017/10/04/the-article-that-made-16000-profs-go-wild/.

189 "Drawing upon Indigenous worldviews": Enrique Galindo and Jill Newton, eds. *Proceedings of the 39th Annual Meeting of the North American Chapter of the International Group for the Psychology of Mathematics Education* (Indianapolis, IN: Hoosier Association of Mathematics Teacher Educators, 2017).

198 The body positivity movement promotes morbidly obese models: Danielle Moores, "Obesity: Causes, Complications, and Diagnosis," *Healthline*, July 16, 2018, www.healthline.com/health/obesity (accessed August 25, 2019).

199 Book by Bradley Campbell and Jason Manning: *The Rise of Victimhood Culture: Microaggressions, Safe Spaces, and the New Culture Wars* (New York: Palgrave Macmillan, 2018).

201 "the natural moral currency of victimhood": See the chapter "False Accusations, Moral Panics and the Manufacture of Victimhood," in Campbell and Manning, *The Rise of Victimhood Culture.*

10 Liberalism as an Alternative to Critical Social Justice

211 "What liberalism has in its favor are the facts": Adam Gopnik, *A Thousand Small Sanities: The Moral Adventure of Liberalism* (London: Riverrun, 2019), 24.

211 "It begins with skepticism": Steven Pinker, *The Better Angels of Our Nature: The Decline of Violence in History and Its Causes* (London: Allen Lane, 2011).

220 "a little less white": Michael Lee, "'Whiteness Studies' Professor to White People: You're Racist If You Don't Judge by Skin Color," *Pluralist*, May 29, 2019, pluralist.com/ robin-diangelo-colorblindness-dangerous/.

ABOUT THE AUTHORS

Helen Pluckrose is a liberal political and cultural writer and the founder of Counterweight (counterweightsupport.com). A participant in the Grievance Studies Affair probe that highlighted problems in Critical Social Justice scholarship, she is today an exile from the humanities, where she researched late medieval and early modern religious writing by and for women. She lives in England and can be found on Twitter @HPluckrose.

James Lindsay is a mathematician with a background in physics and founder of New Discourses (newdiscourses.com). He is interested in the psychology of religion, authoritarianism, and extremism. He led the Grievance Studies Affair probe that made international headlines in 2018, including the front page of the *New York Times*. He lives in Tennessee and can be found on Twitter @ConceptualJames.

Rebecca Christiansen is a novelist and essayist. Her debut YA novel, *Maybe in Paris*, was released in 2017, and she has several popular stories published on Wattpad. She lives in Canada and can be found on Twitter and Wattpad at @rebeccarightnow.